FORGIVE US OUR PRAYERS
THE SECRET OF EFFECTIVE PRAYER

JOHN A. HUFFMAN JR.

John Huffman is a husband, father of three daughters, and a pastor. He has served as pastor of the Key Biscayne Presbyterian Church in Florida, the First Presbyterian Church of Pittsburgh in Pennsylvania, and since 1978 has been the senior minister of the St Andrews Presbyterian Church in Newport Beach, California, a 4,700-member congregation. He has written nine books, numerous articles, and has traveled widely as a speaker and as a board member of WorldVision International, Christianity Today International, and Gordon-Conwell Theological Seminary. His wife Anne is a psychoanalyst.

OUR FATHER IN HEAVEN

HALLOWED BE YOUR NAME

YOUR KINGDOM COME

YOUR WILL BE DONE

ON EARTH AS IT IS IN HEAVEN

GIVE US TODAY OUR DAILY BREAD

FORGIVE US OUR PRAYERS
THE SECRET OF EFFECTIVE PRAYER

AS WE ALSO HAVE FORGIVEN OUR DEBTORS

AND LEAD US NOT INTO TEMPTATION

BUT DELIVER US FROM THE EVIL ONE

JOHN A. HUFFMAN JR.

CHRISTIAN FOCUS

Copyright © John A. Huffman Jr. 2005

ISBN 1-84550-051-2

10 9 8 7 6 5 4 3 2 1

Published in 2005
by
Christian Focus Publications Ltd.,
Geanies House, Fearn, Ross-shire,
IV20 1TW, Scotland, UK

www.christianfocus.com

Cover design by Alister MacInnes

Printed and bound by
Nørhaven Paperback A/S, Denmark

Contents

1
Teach us to Pray

'Lord, teach us to pray'
Luke 11:1

Prayer is basic to our spiritual survival. To stay spiritually healthy, we cannot afford to classify prayer as a low priority item. Discovering new insights about it from God's Word will help us to remember its importance.

All of us come to moments in our lives in which it is important for us to stop, reassess who we are, where we are going, and rediscover the importance of prayer. Although any point in life is a good time to stop and reassess, I'm struck by the appropriateness of doing so now. Some of us became quite self-confident as the stock market moved upward so fast in the 1990s. It was easy to develop a high-tech approach to life, putting our confidence in how smart we were, how clever at picking stocks, and how secure our future would be as a result of our intelligence. But many of us discovered we weren't as smart as we thought we were when our portfolios were caught in the downturn. As a result, we have had to reassess who we are and where we put our trust.

In fact, we've gone from being over-confident to developing second-guessing as an art form. We are not certain what to trust anymore. We hear horrendous news reports of multinational companies collapsing, and we see how much of our reality can be put together with mirrors, making life appear to be what it really is not. We read stories of high-placed executives profiteering in their stock sales at the price of their employees and stockholders. Then we wonder what the next shock wave to hit our culture will be. We've already reeled in shock at the September 11 terrorists' attacks, the war in Iraq, elaborate budget surpluses that have now turned to deficits, and pension schemes that will provide only a fraction of what we expected in retirement. And it may be that your existential realities have come very close to home. They may involve reversals of health, the discovery that your husband is addicted to pornography, fears about the direction your child has chosen to move in life, or the failing health of an aging parent.

It is a good time to stop, reassess where we are, and either discover or rediscover how basic prayer is to our spiritual survival. For we must come at it time and time again, reminding ourselves of its importance, and discovering new insights about it from the Word of God. I invite you to identify with the disciples who specifically asked Jesus to teach them to pray. We will look at His response as it is embodied in what we call the Lord's Prayer, and other comments.

Why Don't we Pray More?

I am convinced that very few of us need to be told once again that we ought to pray. Manipulating people with this sense of 'oughtness' often ends up being counter-productive. However, let me put this question to you. Do you pray enough? I'm not telling you how much you should pray. I'm simply asking you whether or not, in your most honest moments, you have that sense of affirmation that comes from being 'prayed up'. Frankly, I have my own deficiencies in this area. I have to keep asking myself the question, Why do I not pray more? If we reflect on this long enough, I think we would probably come up with three main reasons why we do not pray enough.

Moral Difficulties.

We know that, on occasion, there are moral inequities in our lives that make it impossible to pray. The only way that we can break free into a vital prayer life is to make a decision. We have to choose between our self-will, which drives us into actions and attitudes that are against God's will for our lives, or choose to go his way. It is impossible to have a vital prayer life when our lives are caught up in unconfessed sin. We are called to either give up self or give up prayer. And sometimes we prefer to give up the latter.

Unbelief

At times I struggle with this in my own spiritual life. I have prayed often and intensely about specific needs in my life, and the lives of others, and have not had the answers for which I prayed. So my logical conclusion is, in very subtle and sometimes not-so-subtle ways, to back off from prayer in the self-protective, defensive mood of not wanting to have my hopes and dreams shattered. The lowering of expectations of God and disbelief in his promises can be convenient ways of getting both Him and me off the hook.

External Pressures

A third reason that we do not pray enough is simply that the pressures of the moment crowd out prayer. Perhaps this is the most prevalent reason. How many times have we determined to have a good, healthy quiet time only to have the phone ring, a family difficulty arise, or some other momentary inconvenience interrupt? There is the 'tyranny of the urgent', those momentary inconveniences that distract us from a concentrated conversation with God. Perhaps with advance planning we could eliminate interruptions. By taking the telephone off the hook, or by planning to pray when the house is quiet, time spent with God could be more worthwhile.

Jesus, Man of Prayer

The truth is that we don't pray more because we don't value its importance as much as Jesus did. His life was filled with prayer. Everywhere He went, He went praying. He prayed for His enemies, His friends, His ministry and His physical needs. For Jesus, prayer was as natural as breathing is for us.

I have discovered that whatever my reasons for not praying, periodically I need to back off, take a look at myself, take a look at the biblical teaching about prayer, and, more specifically, take a look at Jesus. This exercise allows me to re-calibrate where I am in my own relationship with God when it comes to prayer. I need to deal with a kind of 'spiritual drift' in which I'm carried by the tides of external circumstances, and my own internal processing of those circumstances, in a way that brings me back to a realistic and honest encounter with the living God, and the dynamic potential available in an active prayer life. I need to remind myself of the many positive answers I've received to prayers in the past, and confront my own unconfessed sin and preoccupation with the urgent, in ways that creatively acknowledge God's grace and continued activity in my life in spite of my own faltering discipleship.

Several times the Bible tells us that Jesus went off by himself to pray:

One of those days Jesus went out into the hills to pray, and spent the night praying to God.

Luke 6:12

One day Jesus was praying in a certain place.

Luke 11:1

After He had dismissed them, He went up into the hills by Himself to pray. When evening came, He was there alone.

Matt. 14:23

After leaving them, He went into the hills to pray.
Mark 6:45

On other occasions He took His inner circle of disciples with him:

Jesus… took Peter, John and James with Him and went up onto a mountain to pray.
Luke 9:28

Then Jesus went with His disciples to a place called Gethsemane, and He said to them, 'Sit here while I go over there and pray.' He took Peter and the two sons of Zebedee along with Him, and He began to be sorrowful and troubled. Then He said to them, 'My soul is overwhelmed with sorrow to the point of death. Stay here and keep watch with me.'

Going a little farther, He fell with His face to the ground and prayed, 'My Father, if it is possible, may this cup be taken from me. Yet not as I will, but as you will.'

Then He returned to His disciples and found them sleeping. 'Could you men not keep watch with me for one hour?' He asked Peter. 'Watch and pray so that you will not fall into temptation. The spirit is willing, but the body is weak.'

He went away a second time and prayed, 'My Father, if it is not possible for this cup to be taken away unless I drink it, may your will be done.'

When He came back, He again found them sleeping, because their eyes were heavy. So He left them and went away once more and prayed the third time, saying the same thing.

Matt. 26:36-44

Look at Jesus. Really look at Him for a moment in his humanity and see how He *modeled prayer*. His was a life of prayer. Everywhere He went, He went praying. He prayed for everything: his enemies, His friends, His style of ministry, His physical needs.

Jesus prayed everywhere, about everything and about everyone. He maintained a constant attitude of prayer. It is exciting to see how He used prayer to cope with complicated situations. If we study his life closely, we will see that, although He prayed at particular moments of crisis, He didn't just wait for that moment to begin his praying. Jesus patterns a prayer life that both anticipates the crisis before it happens and thinks back to it afterwards.

For example, Jesus equipped himself spiritually by spending an occasional entire night in prayer. He did this before choosing the twelve:

At daybreak Jesus went out to a solitary place. The people were looking for Him and when they came to where He was, they tried to stop Him from leaving them (Luke 4:42).

And the calling of the disciples followed just afterwards. The Lord did not just play it by His hunches. In contrast to the Lord, I am afraid that many of us stumble into decisions without having adequately laid a prayer foundation. Decisions, which can shape an entire future, are so often made on the whim of the moment. How much better it would be to set aside a time to call upon the Lord, unpressured by the immediate, simply seeking His will for the long haul.

Not only do some of us neglect praying before a crisis or a particular spiritual battle, I think even more of us are inclined to forget to pray after the battle is over. I have to admit more prayer goes into my preaching before I preach than goes into it afterward. Follow-up prayer is just as important.

Jesus provides an alternative model:

An Alternative Model

Mark records:

> They went to Capernaum and when the Sabbath came, Jesus went into the synagogue and began to teach. The people were amazed at His teaching, because He taught them as one who had authority, not as the teachers of the law. Just then a man in their synagogue, who

was possessed by an evil spirit cried out, 'What do you want with us, Jesus of Nazareth? Have you come to destroy us? I know who you are – the Holy One of God!'

'Be quiet!' said Jesus sternly. 'Come out of him!' The evil spirit shook the man violently and came out of him with a shriek.

The people were all so amazed that they asked each other. 'What is this? A new teaching – and with authority! News about Him spread quickly over the whole region of Galilee.

As soon as they left the synagogue, they went with James and John to the home of Simon and Andrew. Simon's mother-in-law was in bed with a fever, and they told Jesus about her. So He went to her, took her hand and helped her up. The fever left her and she began to wait on them.

That evening after sunset the people brought to Jesus all the sick and demon-possessed. The whole town gathered at the door and Jesus healed many who had various diseases. He also drove out many demons, but He would not let the demons speak because they knew who He was.

Mark 1:21-24

What a day! It began with Jesus teaching in the synagogue and amazing the scribes with His authority. And it ended, after sunset, with the healing of many of local sick and demon-possessed people. Jesus must have been exhausted. You would think He would have slept in late the next morning, wouldn't you?

Mark records:

> *Very early in the morning, while it was still dark, Jesus got up, left the house and went off to a solitary place, where He prayed.*
>
> Mark 1:35

The Lord didn't luxuriate in the past victory. Instead, Jesus knew the need for spiritual resources beyond those of the present. And He was willing to pay the price to find that refurbishment after the struggle, as well as in anticipation of the new ministries of the next day.

In his gift of prayer God has given us a tremendous spiritual resource and has modeled it through Christ's own ministry. Not only do we understand prayer from the content of his prayers, but also from the life of prayer that He lived before the world. The disciples had observed Jesus at prayer and wanted to learn to pray too. If we are genuinely joined with the disciples in spirit – if we also want to learn to pray – the Lord will teach us. But we must be willing to follow his guidance, or we will stumble on, praying our somewhat ineffectual prayers.

The Centrality of Prayer

One of my concerns for the church of our day is my impression that we are really not the praying church we should be and can be. This doesn't mean that we don't pray. I know that many of us have our own prayer discipline. I'm talking about the church genuinely interceding for the work of Jesus Christ. Part of my own congregation's Vision Statement includes these words:

> We confess the Lordship of Jesus Christ over our church and over our individual lives, and we commit ourselves to growing in maturity as His disciples. As we give more of ourselves to Christ, *we pray that as a church we might increase our dependence on prayer,* become more intentional about encouraging others in discipleship, exhibit more joy and become known for the ways in which we celebrate the Lord in praise and worship.

Prayer is central in this vision.

A Spiritual Resource

We live in a day in which we hear a great deal about the 'user-friendly church'. Churches try to offer programs that meet everyone's needs. It is so easy for each of us to interface with this ministry at the point at which we get our needs serviced, and then perhaps criticize that part that does not relate to us in our immediate need. We can critique preaching, critique the music, critique the youth program, critique what we are or are not doing for singles. We can analyze the personalities of the clergy and the lay leadership. We can have our varied opinions about where our denomination is going or where it should go. We come with our own agendas. That is natural. That is normal. The question is, is prayer for our fellowships, as communities of followers of Jesus, part of that agenda? Is there an urgency in prayer that precedes anything we do and follows up anything that, by God's grace, we have accomplished?

Some years ago, a preacher was sent to a community to serve a church that he described as being 'little more than a wreck'. His predecessor, a very popular man, had been forced to leave the leadership of that church, and the ministry, because of a scandal. As a result, the congregation was divided and the church greatly discredited. After looking over the situation, the new pastor decided that a real spiritual awakening was the only hope. He undertook to do the preaching but, at the same time, he invited a layman whom he knew to be mighty in prayer, to assist him in his public efforts by his secret prayers. For ten days of special services the preacher labored, apparently in vain. On the tenth night, the layman came in with a radiant face to announce the coming victory. The preacher, Clovis G. Chappell, never forgot the service that followed. It marked the beginning of a new day in that church and, to some extent, in the entire community. The real battle was won in advance through prayer. Chappell declared, 'All we did in the actual service was to gather the spoils which had been won in the place of prayer.'

God has given us a tremendous spiritual resource. He models it through Christ's own ministry. He calls you to prayer; He calls me to prayer. The problem with us preachers is that *we tell you to pray, but we do not teach you to pray.* The title of this chapter could have been worded in a slightly different way. It could have read, 'Lord, teach us how to pray.' That request has a familiar, biblical ring to us. But it is not quite accurate.

Scripture tells us that on one occasion, Jesus was praying. When He ceased His private time of prayer, one of His disciples said to Him:

Lord, teach us to pray, just as John taught his disciples'.

Luke 11:1

Although the question sounds about the same, there is a difference. The disciples omitted one word that we are apt to insert - the word is 'how'. The disciples had observed Jesus at prayer. They wanted to learn to do it, not just how to do it. One of Satan's clever tactics is to get us Christians bogged down in discussions on 'how' to pray. He can even get us to the point where we quarrel about it. What we need is to learn to actually pray.

Praying Incorrectly

Our need for Jesus teaching us how to pray is underlined as the Bible makes it clear that we can pray incorrectly. James puts it in these words:

You want something but don't get it. You kill and covet, but you cannot have what you want. You quarrel and fight. You do not have, because you do not ask God. When you ask, you do not receive, because you ask with wrong motives, that you may spend what you get on your pleasures'.

James 4:2-3

If we remain uneducated in prayer, we can be like a little child who keeps begging for candy. He loves the taste. He knows what he wants. When his mother gives him carrot sticks and celery instead of candy, he gets angry. He so much prefers the taste of candy. Little does he realize how it can rot his teeth. Little does he realize the nutritional value of vegetables over candy. In our undisciplined, adult prayer lives we often beg from God those things that can destroy, and resent His failure to give them. We had better learn to pray the way Jesus would have us pray, so that our prayers will not become self-perpetuated ego trips.

The disciples wanted to learn from Jesus, which is why the made their request, 'Lord, teach us to pray…' It was this that evoked what we now call the Lord's Prayer. Jesus' model prayer came to people expressing their need to know how to pray.

A Brief, Childlike Prayer

Pious Jews prayed three times each day. Their prayers included eighteen petitions and their normal, memorized prayer was three times as long as the Lord's Prayer. Jesus was not intending to teach His disciples one prayer that they would memorize, and to which they would then limit themselves for the rest of their lives. Instead, He was warning against a babbling, hypocritical prayer style in which we try to convince others of our piety. Brevity that is sincere is of greater value than verbosity planned for effect. We think we will impress God and others with long theological prayers, but the only ones who will be impresses are ourselves.

Jesus, the Teacher, instead of giving a philosophical discourse on the nature of prayer, responded with these words, 'When you pray, say: …' Then He actually prayed, giving them a straightforward and understandable model:

> *Our Father, hallowed be Your name,*
> *Your kingdom come.*
> *Give us each day our daily bread.*
> *Forgive us our sins*
> *For we also forgive everyone who sins against us.*
> *And lead us not into temptation.*

Luke 11:2-4

'Father' acknowledges a childlike posture. It implies a helplessness, which a dependent has before an all-powerful parent. And it implies a relationship of trust. How refreshing it is to come humbly before our Creator, the One who has all power.

'Hallowed be your name' acknowledges our willingness to humbly bow in adoration as finite beings before the infinite God.

'Your kingdom come' places us, the creature, back at the feet of the Creator, implies that we are interested in his kingdom, not our kingdom, expressing our willingness to adapt our dreams and wishes to his dreams and wishes.

'Give us each day our daily bread' expresses our need for His daily provision, implies that we believe that every good and perfect gift comes from God.

'Forgive us our sins, for we also forgive everyone who sins against us' makes a clear statement of the reciprocal nature of our need for forgiveness and our need to forgive others.

'And lead us not into temptation' emphasizes our desire to avoid those situations that lend themselves to sin. In these simple words we are asking God to help us in our struggle with temptation and to be proactive in leading us in ways that minimize our bent toward sin. This acknowledges the reality of the Evil One and our need for protection in our daily spiritual warfare.

It takes only 30 seconds to say this prayer and its more elaborate expression recorded in Matthew. We can reel it off without ever thinking. In my early years in our congregation, we prayed it practically every Sunday. In more recent years, we have varied the pace, not praying it every week so that when we do pray the Lord's Prayer we will be reminded to take it more seriously. It is important that we ponder its power that we refuse to say it so quickly and so tritely. Remember, it demonstrates what prayer is all about.

I need a model. I need someone to teach me to pray. I often find myself confused when I try to do something without the right kind of modeling, without a practical, hands-on kind of instruction. Some years ago, I bought a toy as a birthday present for one of our daughters. I got it home and about had a nervous breakdown trying to assemble it. The instructions telling me how to put it together were complete. The diagrams were correct. All the parts were there. The problem was I had no one to show me how to do it. About the same time, Anne and I bought a brand-new vacuum cleaner. What a different experience. The salesman came into our living room. He demonstrated how to use the machine. We never looked at the directions because his demonstration was so thorough. We should pray the Lord's Prayer, and model after it. It is so simple and straightforward, yet profound.

Daring Prayer

When Jesus taught His disciples to pray, He didn't destroy the old prayers they had prayed before. He simply brought in new dimensions.

If we take this prayer seriously, it will change our lives radically. Take, for example, the phrase 'Thy will be done.' Do we really mean that? Do we truly want God's will done in our lives? Wouldn't it be more honest to say we want Him to help us get our will for our lives? We know what we want. We know what is best for us. We have the script already written. In fact, we get angry when God doesn't come in on cue. We want Him to do what we want Him to do when we want Him to do it. And He seems to be so stubborn, insisting on His will, not ours.

Wait a minute! That is why Jesus taught them to pray. He had that corrective that even today transforms lives. He is saying, 'Let God be God. Obey Him.' Let His will be ours, not our will be His. In fact, he is telling us to so desire His will that ultimately our wills become molded into conformity with His.

The Lord's Prayer begins with the name of God. In personal terms, we approach Him as a father. We acknowledge His sovereignty over us as one who is in heaven. We treat Him with reverence. We combine our personal familiarity with the distinct sense of who He is. It is a prayer that progresses to adoration and surrender to His will. We hallow His name. We call for His kingdom to come. We want His will. And we call upon Him to provide our necessities of daily bread and forgiveness, and we acknowledgment our weakness and our need for deliverance from evil.

Do you catch the symmetry that Jesus brings to this model? When we have ingrained into our deepest understanding this balanced attitude toward prayer, we are released to pray about anything and everything that comes our way.

Luke finds it only natural to proceed to some further comments Jesus made about prayer. These comments were not part of the Lord's Prayer. They were a natural outgrowth of it. Jesus tells about a friend who needs to feed a midnight visitor. The man goes to the home of his friend at midnight, knocks at the door and, awakening him, says,

> *'Friend, lend me three loaves of bread, because a friend of mine on a journey has come to me, and I have nothing to set before him'.*
>
> Luke 11:5-6

Jesus muses about the thoughts which the person just awakened must be having. He could very well answer,

> *'Don't bother me. The door is already locked, and my children are with me in bed. I can't get up and give you anything'.*
>
> Luke 11:7

27

The Lord says, in fact, that's not the answer He will give. He says:

> *I tell you, though he will not get up and give him the bread because he is his friend, yet because of the man's boldness he will get up and give him as much as he needs.*

Luke 11:8

Jesus is telling this story to first-century Jews for whom the notion of our contemporary individualism was quite foreign. He was talking in the Middle Eastern paradigm, not a Western paradigm. The key to this little story is the word 'boldness'. It was because of this man's boldness that the friend felt an obligation to get up and be of help.

You see, a person who arrived at night was not just a guest of the individual in whose home he was staying. He was also a guest of the community. This notion of communal responsibility is so foreign to our Western mind-set. The fact is that if this man refused to get up and help service the needs of this community guest, the story would be all over the community. He was willing to help because he desired to avoid the shame that would come from the negative reflection on his character.

The Character of God

This passage teaches something about the character of God. God's very name and honor are involved in hearing the prayers of His people. Jesus teaches that, based on the very character of God, we can be assured of an answer to our prayers. God has invested Himself in us. And God wants to bring His will to earth. We are simply disobedient if we do not talk very frankly to the Father. It is His business to answer, bringing His will to earth, not just to do what we want. We are privileged to place ourselves in the very hands of the God of the universe and to believe that His character demands that He take seriously our requests, answering them in ways He knows is best. Jesus continues this teaching on prayer, instructing us:

> *So I say to you: Ask and it will be given to you; seek and you will find; knock and the door will be opened to you. For everyone who asks receives; he who seeks finds; and to him who knocks, the door will be opened.*

Luke 11:9-10

It's a powerful promise, isn't it? The very God of the universe has instructed us to call upon Him persistently. Once again He appeals to the character of God when He states:

Which of you fathers, if your son asks for a fish, will give him a snake instead? Or if he asks for an egg, will give him a scorpion? If you then, though you are evil, know how to give good gifts to your children, how much more will your Father in heaven give the Holy Spirit to those who ask him!

Luke 11:11-13

Our heavenly Father will give us what is best if we come to Him, genuinely desiring His best. If you have walked with Jesus in the past, if you are attracted by all the potentialities of His divine/human nature, I urge you to pause, as did His disciples, and to put your request to Him, 'Lord, teach us to pray…'

I've walked many a mile with Jesus. And I've walked some without Him. I will assure you that the way gets pretty lonely when we willingly choose to disengage ourselves from that daily, frequent, ongoing conversation with our Lord. I urge you, as I urge myself, to talk frankly with Him and to expect Him to answer our prayers as we probe more and more deeply into those model words:

Our Father, in heaven, hallowed be your name, your kingdom come, your will be done on earth as it is in heaven. Give us today our daily bread. Forgive us our debts, as we have forgiven

*our debtors. And lead us not into temptation,
but deliver us from the evil one, for yours is the
kingdom and the power and the glory, forever.
Amen.*

Matt. 6:9-13

2
Our Heavenly Father

'Jesus said, 'This is how you should pray:
'Our Father in heaven...'
Matthew 6:9

An artist was trying to depict Niagara Falls. If you've been there, you'll understand the problem he had. The setting is so majestic. Suddenly, he threw down his brush in despair. The rainbow, the wonder, and the majesty of the foam defied him. How could he possibly hope to capture, in paint, the unending roar?

The Lord's Prayer is even more awesome. It would be as difficult to do it justice as to try to capture the Niagara Falls on canvas. However, fortunately, we have it before us. We can point to it. We can observe it as a model given by Jesus Himself. We can read it, think about it, recite it, sing it and learn from it. Realizing that, when we have done all of these things, there will still be more to learn and experience.

Back to Niagara Falls. There are many who live in that part of the world who, when they are wondering how to entertain guests, think, 'We have friends visiting us, and we're going to have to take them to the Falls tomorrow.' We've all experienced how familiarity breeds contempt. In this case, familiarity breeds familiarity, a kind of lessening of appreciation. Every time I've gone on an extensive world trip, I've come back to Newport Beach with a much greater sense of appreciation for the beauty of the environment in which we live and the privileges we have as citizens of democracies. It takes being away from our natural habitat to come back and have a greater appreciation it.

It's the same with the Lord's Prayer. We've memorized it. We've said it hundreds of times. In some churches it is said at every service. We can say it so quickly that the words come out faster than our mind is able to comprehend what we're saying. It's like the Niagara Falls to a person who lives in Buffalo. As you read this book, I hope you will join me in taking a fresh look at the Lord's Prayer. Pretend you've never read, heard, sung, or recited the words before.

Prayer, an Inexpensive Therapy?

Every so often I run into a cynic who tips his hat toward religion. He'll acknowledge that it has had a positive effect upon some people. He will even grant that prayer can be helpful. There's only one problem. This skeptic doesn't believe there's anything to religion except for its self-delusionary impact on the person who practices it. The same would go for prayer. Prayer, he thinks, is a positive force if it helps us coordinate our thoughts. It gives us a good chance to talk through a problem, or to find that penetrating insight into an issue that concerns us. The fact that the cynic thinks there is no God is incidental. He also feels religion can increase your contentment level, that prayer can give personal insight. In fact, he says it is the least expensive form of therapy.

Jesus destroyed this one-dimensional, pragmatic approach to religion in many ways. In particular, He did it by modeling the Lord's Prayer for His disciples. Luke tells us that the disciples said to Him,

'Lord, teach us to pray...'

Luke 11:1

Matthew tells us that Jesus answered their request by saying,

> *This, then, is how you should pray: 'Our Father in heaven...*

Matt. 6:9

When we say 'Our Father in heaven,' we are engaged in more than self-encouragement. We are exposing ourselves to some very special realities about ourselves and about God.

An Ongoing, Personal Relationship with God

The Lord's Prayer begins with a personal pronoun. Prayer is not a formalistic expression although we can make it that. We can recite our prayers with the cold formality with which we recite a nursery rhyme. Or we can expose ourselves to that personal dimension in which we genuinely express ourselves.

I've observed husbands and wives who have a mechanical relationship. She fulfills her role. He fulfills his. They do what they should do with a minimum of personal interaction. They have a formal relationship. Every so often the wife will question her pastor or a therapist as to how she can get her husband to open up at a personal level. He's a good man. He does everything he should. He works hard and he brings home his paycheck. He simply doesn't share himself, personally, with her or with their children. It's frustrating to be engaged in a one-way personal relationship. The wife yearns to be touched by her partner's feelings. She wants to enter into a conversation, to feel his presence. Perhaps it's the other way round. The wife has sealed herself off from her husband. He is the one who yearns for a greater intimacy. Often, both share the same feelings but do not know how to express them.

God yearns to have a personal relationship with us. He expresses himself through the Scriptures with a high degree of intimacy. He wants conversation. How sad it is if we're like a young man I read about who ran out of money in a strange city. He didn't have so much as a penny. This was in the day before credit cards. He walked the streets hungry. Although he passed hundreds of people, he asked none of them for help. It wasn't that he didn't have a great need. He genuinely needed money. The problem was that everyone he passed was a stranger. He was fearful that they would not care to help. So the hunger pangs grew as he shuffled on alone, suffering in silence.

Some of us act the same way toward God. We walk through life with tremendous needs. Perhaps we don't believe in God. Even if we do, we see Him sealed off from us. Somehow He seems to be inaccessible. Somehow we sense that He is unavailable and unconcerned. The Lord's Prayer models how to talk to a God who does care. We can have a personal relationship with Him. We can pray it right now and expect to be heard by God. Pray with an open attitude. Pray, repentant for sin. Pray, expecting to be heard by the personal God who created us in His image.

The great Jewish theologian, philosopher Martin Buber was well known for the way in which he distinguished between 'I–It' relationships and 'I–Thou' relationships. We have an 'I–It' relationship with a table, a chair, a car, a tennis racket, or a broom. We have an 'I–Thou' relationship with someone we deeply love and with whom we have an open-hearted intimacy. Buber makes it quite clear that we can function in an 'I–It' relationship with the God of all creation, seeing God as distant and impersonal. If that's our view of God, it's going to seriously impair our prayer life. Instead, if we have an 'I–Thou' relationship with God, seeing him in personal terms, it transforms how we pray.

Individual and Corporate Prayer.

One of my friends, Jon Healey, gave me this statement about the Lord's Prayer:

*You cannot pray The Lord's Prayer and even
once say 'I',*
   *You cannot pray The Lord's Prayer and even
once say 'My'.*
   When you pray, you pray for one another,
   *When you ask for daily bread, you must
include your brother.*
   For others are included in each and every plea,
   From beginning to end it does not once say 'ME'.

Although we are entitled to pray the Lord's
Prayer as individuals, it has to it a great
corporate significance.

Jesus did not teach a hermit-type faith.
I remember working on a building and grounds
crew in Northern Indiana each summer during
my junior high and high school days. Every so
often we would take a pick-up truck full of junk
to the city dump. There was an old hermit there.
He was unkempt. We didn't want to stand down-
wind of him. He apparently seldom showered or
changed his clothes. When he saw us coming, he
shuffled off to the side into a makeshift shack,
doing his best to be inconspicuous. We dumped
our load and drove away. Through the dust
we could see him go directly to what we had
dumped and begin to rifle through our junk,
looking for items of interest. This sad man was
a loner. This hermit lived independent of other
people. What a sad existence.

In a somewhat similar way, we can try to go it alone in our prayer life. While prayer can be powerful in its individualistic form, it takes on a magnificent, complementary dynamic when it is corporate. Jesus talked about two or three people being gathered together in His name. He talked about prayer being done in community. True, He spent some of His nights alone in prayer. True, He urged His followers to go into their closets and shut the door, praying in private. The point Jesus made was that prayer was not a public ritual to impress other people. It's a conversation between us and God.

But that closed door did not imply that others cannot be with us behind that closed door. The issue is, what is our attitude in prayer? Is our involvement with other people to be seen by them or to share with them in an earnest, sincere, community act?

Jesus said:

> *Again, I tell you that if two of you on earth agree about anything you ask for, it will be done for you by My Father in heaven. For where two or three come together in My name, there am I with them'.*

Matt. 18:19-20

Jesus didn't teach them to pray, saying, 'My Father.' He said, 'Our Father.' We are not 'only children.' Too much of our prayer life makes us sound like only children. Jesus models for us what it is to pray as a member of a family.

There is power in such corporate prayer. Great revivals have grown out of prayer meetings. A healthy church is one that has a concentration on corporate prayer. Jesus made this clear by using the plural pronoun in conjunction with God when He modeled for us the opening words 'Our Father'. Joining a prayer group can be exciting. I remember the Sunday afternoon prayer meetings at First Presbyterian Church in Pittsburgh where we shared together as we brought out mutual concerns to God. It was a group effort. We prayed about specific needs – and God answered in specific ways.

When we think about prayer being done in community, let's remember that our community is larger than our personal preferences. There are a lot more people in a right relationship with God than we might be inclined to believe. How exciting it is to be involved in a prayer group where there is a variety of personality types. How good it is to gather as the people of God, bringing our specific requests. It's community. We are sharing together. There is power in this sharing process as we bring our mutual concerns to God.

This is why, in my own congregation, prayer is a very important part of our covenant groups, why we have our prayer telephone line. This is why elders are available in the prayer room after every worship service to pray with people about whatever needs they have. This is why we have, once a year, the 24-Hour Prayer Vigil. I have such satisfying memories of coming over to the church for one of those hours in the middle of the night, being in a circle with brothers and sisters in Jesus Christ, each of us having several cards in our hands representing the hundreds of cards filled out by those with specific prayer requests. This is why we have prayer teams that go into homes and into hospitals to pray with the sick. This is why we have a group of elders and staff meeting together on Saturdays and Sundays, prior to our worship services, to claim God's power in this ministry. That's why in our Session meetings, when needs arise, we stop, and two or three elders pray specifically for that need. And when the prayer is answered, a meeting or two or three later, we will stop and thank God for the answer to prayer.

Praying to our Father

It is not true to say that Jesus was the first one to use the term 'Father' in relationship to God. This title occurs in the Old Testament, though not used in prayer. Jesus was not the first one to use the term *Father* in that way. The term was used several times in Isaiah:

> *But you are our Father, though Abraham does not know us, or Israel acknowledge us; you, O Lord, art our Father, our Redeemer from of old is your name.*
>
> Isa. 63:16

Later Isaiah wrote:

> *Yet, O Lord, you are our Father. We are the clay, you are the potter.*
>
> Isa. 64:8

God referred to Israel as being His sons:

> *For the Lord has spoken: 'I reared children and brought them up, but they have rebelled against me'.*
>
> Isa. 1:2

We are told that in the inter-testamental period, as in the time of Jesus, Jewish prayers were occasionally addressed to God as Father. However, rarely would a Jew pray, 'My Father' or 'Our Father'. It was appropriate only on the lips of the most saintly person. Up to that point, God was not viewed in quite the same personal terms. The Greeks prayed to 'father Zeus', though that was void of close, personal connotations. It was a name of honor for a god who ranked high in the gallery of gods.

Jesus radicalized prayer by urging ordinary, earthly persons to say, 'Our Father'. Just imagine the impact of this teaching. According to Jewish traditional, certain names of God were not even spoken. When the Hebrew word *Jehovah* appeared in the text, Jewish readers would, out of reverence, substitute the word *Adonai*. The Holy God was to be treated with the utmost reverence. Here Jesus is talking about Him in as intimate terms as we could imagine. Jesus came to reveal the Father. He said on another occasion:

> *All things have been committed to me by my Father. No one knows the Son except the Father, and no one knows the Father except the Son and those to whom the Son chooses to reveal Him'.*

Matt. 11:27

This personal dynamic of praying to God as Father was vividly driven home to me a number of years ago when I was visiting Israel. I was staying in what was then the Jerusalem Hilton Hotel, a tall cylindrical building more than twenty stories high. I was waiting for an elevator when I discovered that one of them was broken, stuck between two floors. I heard an anguished cry wafting down through that long elevator shaft. It was a cry of a little boy all alone and helpless and crying out, 'Abba! Abba! Abba!' He was crying out in the most personal terms for whom? He was crying out, 'Daddy! Daddy! Daddy!' He was using the intimate Hebrew word that Jesus must have used for Father.

Every time I pray the Lord's Prayer I think of the revolutionary dynamic Jesus brought to prayer, giving us personal, direct, relational access to the Creator/Sustainer God, to a highly personal understanding Father. Now, this has explosive potential depending on how we perceive a father to function. If you've had a good relationship with your earthly father, you'll find it much easier to understand the intimate, personal dynamic that Jesus is modeling for us.

I am aware that there are some who will read this whose fathers made an earthly hell out of their homes. If you are among them, it may be that the last thing you want to do is think of God as a father. When you do, it produces only a negative connotation, not something helpful and nurturing. Sadly there are fathers who have violated their moral responsibilities to their children.

I talked with a friend just recently who is yearning to feel closer to God. As we scratched beneath the surface, it became apparent that although her human parents were persons to admire in many ways, they somehow belonged to a generation of parents who lived at an emotional distance from their children. Her father, in particular, put on her expectations that she felt she could never meet. And, in the process, these feelings were transferred to God. Other Scriptural metaphors for God will probably be more helpful to her.

Dr. Armand Nicholi is a Harvard psychiatrist who has done some fascinating research involving father-child relationships. Remember the riots at Harvard University that took place during the late 1960s? Careful research involving some of his patients, who were participants in those riots, revealed confused attitudes toward authority. Harvard University, the police, the government—all became identified with severe parental authority. There was a reaction against authority that was perceived to be heavy-handed. His more recent studies reveal a shift in the problem. Now the problems tend to involve the absence of authority. So-called freedom produces its problems. We find persons who don't know how to handle the absence of a father, whether that father is absent because of divorce or simply absent through business travel, or emotional preoccupation with other matters. It is understandable why many in our society have problems with father imagery.

First Century Fatherhood

When Jesus used this term 'Father', the first century Jewish community knew precisely what He meant. The role of a father was clearly understood. 'Our Father' was an individual and corporate personal address to one who has authority. Judaism was a patriarchal culture. This is evident in the Passover celebration. The Father, as the acknowledged head of the home, would recount the story of Israel's redemption, the exodus from Egypt and the safe crossing of the Red Sea. He presided at the feast, and the Father blessed the unleavened bread and the chalice. The term 'Our Father' didn't have the slightest hint of easy indulgence. It was void of that casual, flippant tone in which some today might query, 'How's your old man?'

To address one's father was to address someone with reverence, with respect, with obedience. The father's posture was that of a loving, caring person who knew his child. The Jewish father was not an absentee landlord. He was responsible for raising his children in the very statutes of the Lord. He was to walk with them in the way. He was to talk with them and tell them about the things of God. He was to be concerned for their welfare. He was to identify the needs of his children. So Jesus makes the reference to the fact that even as earthly fathers provide for their children who come to them in need, so will our heavenly Father make provision for us. He will not turn us away. Even as an earthly father does not dare to spare the rod and spoil the child, so our heavenly Father has an eye for discipline. Even as our earthly father protects us, so our heavenly Father pities those who fear Him.

David wrote:

> *As a father has compassion on his children, so the Lord has compassion on those who fear Him; for He knows how we are formed, He remembers that we are dust'.*

Ps. 103:13-14

He's concerned about those who respond to Him in faith. So, we come to our Father knowing that even before we pray He identifies with us in our need. We come, knowing that even when we have given our requests He knows better than we do what we most need.

Let me share with you a little sideline vignette, a story about a stock boy and a checkout girl. In a supermarket, the stock boy was busy working when a new voice came over the intercom asking for a carry-out at check register four. He was almost finished, and wanted to get some fresh air, so he decided to answer the call. As he approached the check-out stand, a distant smile caught his eye. The new check-out girl was beautiful. She was an older woman, maybe 26, and he was only 22. He fell in love with her right then. Later that day, after his shift was over, he waited by the punch clock to find out her name. She came into the break room, smiled softly at him and took her time card and punched out, then left. He looked at her card and saw her name.

Next day, he waited outside as she left the supermarket and offered to run her home in his car. He looked harmless enough, and she accepted. When he dropped her off, he asked if he could see her again, outside of work. She simply said it wasn't possible. He pressed, and she explained that she was a single parent, had two children and couldn't afford a baby-sitter. So he offered to pay for the baby-sitter. Reluctantly, she accepted his offer for a date the following Saturday.

That Saturday night he arrived at her door only to have her tell him that she was unable to go with him because the baby-sitter had called and canceled. The young man simply said, 'Well, let's take the kids with us.' She tried to explain that taking the children was not an option. But, not taking no for an answer, he pressed. Finally she brought him inside to meet her children. She had an older daughter who was just cute as could be, he thought. Then she brought out her son in a wheelchair. He was born a paraplegic with Down Syndrome. 'I still don't understand why the kids can't come with us,' he said, to the young mother's amazement. Most men would run away from a woman with two kids, especially if one had disabilities. That's just what her husband, the father of her children, had done.

That evening the pair loaded up the kids, went to dinner and the movies. When her son needed anything, the young man took care of him. When he needed to use the rest room, he picked him up out of his chair, took him, and brought him back. The kids loved him. At the end of the evening, that mother knew this was the man she wanted to marry and spend the rest of her life with. A year later, they were married, and their new father adopted both children. Since then they have added two more kids.

I personally find this story quite inspiring, and especially so since it is a true-life story of a well-known American professional football quarterback, who led St Louis Rams to their

Superbowl championship. Such compassion is rare today.

Praying to the Father

Even beyond the very earthly qualities that can be ascribed to God, this Father is different. He is our heavenly Father. He is the transcendent, all-powerful, sovereign God. Jesus prays, 'Our Father in heaven…'

God is our Father by Creation
The Apostle Paul declared to the pagan philosophers on Mars Hill in Athens that we are the offspring of God. We did not happen by chance. He observed there was an inscription 'to the Unknown God'. He declared that God to them.

Luke records in the book of Acts:

Paul then stood up in the meeting of the Areopagus and said: 'Men of Athens! I see that in every way you are very religious. For as I walked round and observed your objects of worship, I even found an altar with this inscription: TO AN UNKNOWN GOD. Now what you worship as unknown I am going to proclaim to you. The God who made the world and everything in it is the Lord of heaven and earth and does not live in temples made by human hands, as if He needed anything, because He Himself gives all men life and breath and everything else… For in Him we live and move and have our being'.

Acts 17:22-25, 28

God is our Father as Redeemer

Some say that the Lord's Prayer is not a prayer for Christians because it doesn't give any specific statements in terms of Christ's atoning work. The early church didn't feel this way about it. So seriously did it take the understanding of what it is to know God as Father that they only allowed baptized persons to repeat it. We are His adopted sons and daughters. Paul states it in these words:

For you did not receive a spirit that makes you a slave again to fear, but you received the Spirit of sonship. And by him we cry, 'Abba, Father.' The Spirit himself testified with our spirit that we are God's children.

Rom. 8:15-16

God is our Father by Providence and Preservation

We have the privilege of being a participant in His plan for us as individuals and for His whole creation. It is important as we contemplate God as Father that we reflect both on the intimate, personal acceptance which that implies, and also pause to realize His transcendent holiness so we do not enter into His presence with a casual attitude. We come with a reverence and respect that is due to a sovereign leader, combined with the sensitive tenderness that we feel toward a loving, compassionate parent.

There's a fascinating phrase in the Book of Acts. Paul, a prisoner for preaching Christ, was sailing for Rome. As the ship passed along the island of Crete, a tempestuous northeaster struck the sea. The ship was violently storm-tossed. The crew began to throw the cargo overboard. Paul called out to the men to listen to him, to take heart, because he had just had a message from the Lord. He said:

> Last night an angel of the God whose I am and whom I serve stood beside me and said, 'Do not be afraid, Paul. You must stand trial before Caesar; and God has graciously given you the lives of all who sail with you.
>
> Acts 27:23-24

There are many messages in this passage. But the phrase that fascinates me reads: '…the God whose I am and whom I serve…' So often we come to God as if we own Him. Far from that, He owns us. We are called to worship Him, not expect that He will bow before our thrones.

Many people say that they live by the Sermon on the Mount, without realizing what that fully means. Jesus said:

> For I tell you that unless your righteousness surpasses that of the Pharisees and the teachers of the law, you will certainly not enter the kingdom of heaven'.
>
> Matt. 5:20

Jesus told a story about a Pharisee and a sinner at prayer:

> Two men went up to the temple to pray, one a Pharisee and the other a tax collector. The Pharisee stood up and prayed about himself: 'God, I thank you that I am not like all other men – robbers, evildoers, adulterers – or even like this tax collector. I fast twice a week and give a tenth of all I get.
>
> But the tax collector stood at a distance. He would not even look up to heaven, but beat his breast and said, 'God, have mercy on me, a sinner.'
>
> I tell you that this man, rather than the other, went home justified before God. For everyone who exalts himself will be humbled, and he who humbles himself will be exalted.
>
> Luke 18:10-14

We should realize that the Pharisee was a man of great dedication to God. He faithfully attended religious services. He prayed regularly and tithed. And he was not an adulterer. All of these were commendable attributes. But Jesus turned to the poor sinner who humbly approached God, begging for compassion and mercy, and said that the sinner was forgiven (Luke 18:9-14).

Our self-righteousness does not impress God. He knows we need the imputed righteousness that comes as we humble ourselves like the sinner in the story. We must acknowledge our sins, claiming the forgiveness and the redemption that is ours because of Christ.

No Pit too Deep

I was privileged to know and love Corrie ten Boom. (The book and film entitled *The Hiding Place* tells her story.) Corrie was an heroic Dutch Christian who, along with her family, saved over 700 Jewish people from Nazi extermination. Her father and brother died in prison. Her nephew disappeared. She and her sister were sent to the Ravensbruck concentration camp. Her sister died there. Due to a clerical error, Corrie was released from the camp and all the horrors of those terrible years. She spent the rest of her life writing and speaking about Jesus.

On one occasion I interviewed Corrie ten Boom on my Pittsburgh TV show. I brought up the topic of suffering and how it was that a good God allowed it. She said, 'No pit is so deep that He (God) is not deeper still.' She pulled out of her bag a piece of needlework she was finishing and held up the reverse side of it for me to see, and for the camera to home in on. 'What is this?' Corrie asked. It looked like a tangle of loose threads. Then she turned it over and showed me the front. It was a beautiful gold crown on a rich, blue background. Corrie then concluded, 'Our loving Father in heaven is preparing a crown for all who trust Him. Sometimes all we see are the tangled, loose threads on the back side of His work. One day we will see the finished product of what He is doing in us!'

Our prayer is individually personal; it is corporately personal. It is addressed to our Father who has authority, our Father who is loving, our Father who is holy. We are privileged to approach Him as sons and daughters. We are entitled to pray as members of the family. How special it is to have this relationship with God and to know that He is intimately interested in each one of us!

When we pray, we say, 'Our Father in heaven!' And we never grow jaded in our sense of the grandeur of that reality!

3
God's Name, God's Kingdom and God's Will

Jesus said, 'This, then, is how you should pray:
'Our Father in heaven,
hallowed be your name,
your kingdom come,
your will be done
on earth as it is in heaven'
Matt. 6:9-10

Words are cheaper by the dozen. Our fast-paced communication networks bombard us with words. Los Angeles alone has over 100 radio stations. We can select whatever set of audio words we want at no charge. Satellite and cable TV increases the possibilities exponentially. If we were to read every word in the *New York Times*, we would not have time for much else.

When the disciples asked Jesus to teach them to pray, they were not just asking for a form of words. They knew a lot of words and had memorized prayers since boyhood. What they wanted was to be certain that they were using the right words in the right way with the right attitude. So Jesus gave them a model. His opening words showed them how they could have individual, personal access to God. By adding the plural pronoun 'our', Jesus stressed the corporate, communal nature of prayer directed to a loving, heavenly Father who, in His intimate concern for His children, continues to command His position of ultimate authority.

Now Jesus teaches how to pray in a three-fold petition that takes the conversation away from ourselves and focuses our attention on Almighty God. This model prayer begins where every prayer should begin. It begins with *adoration* – '*Hallowed by Your name.*' We must never forget that. How flippantly we can address the Sovereign Being who created and sustains everything that exists. How egocentric we can be. Jesus sets that straight from the very beginning. Although there will be times in which the pressing, momentary needs drive us into immediate prayers for ourselves, or for someone in great need, or for an urgent problem that has just arisen, adoration should be our initial, prayerful thrust.

Jesus stressed the word 'your'. Every prayer, by its very nature, should lift us into the very presence of Almighty God. 'Hallowed be *Your* name, *Your* kingdom come, *Your* will be done on earth as it is in heaven.' As self-centered as I am, I hallow my name. I want my kingdom to come. I want my will to be done. Can you relate to my confession? It's basically our fallen human nature to be more interested in me and mine than the very God who created us. In the process, we knock off kilter not only the symmetry of prayer but the very balance of our existence.

Having made these introductory remarks, we now focus on the three adoration statements.

When you Pray, say, 'Hallowed be your Name.'

What does it mean to hallow? On another occasion, Jesus recasts the statement into the direct imperative 'Father, glorify Your name!' (John 12:28). God is being asked to sanctify His very name and to cause humankind to bow before it. The whole endeavor here is to bring glory, honor, and adoration to the God of all history. It is a name made sacred. It is a prayer of consecration. It lifts us above our commonplace, secular, temporal existence into the dimension of eternity.

This raises another question. Just what is there in a name that is so important? When Jesus prayed, 'Hallowed be Your name,' He communicated much more to the Jewish mind than it communicates to us today. To us, a name is a dog tag. We try to pick pleasant sounding names for our children. We can almost tell how old a person is by the name they bear. Particular names come in and out of fashion. It would be interesting to know the number of Jacquelines born in the early 1960s, as compared to that name's usage in the early '50s or early '80s. Our names are sort of code signs for the mailman. They are our computer numbers, our personal zip codes that differentiate us from all the other people in the area.

For the Hebrew people names carried a much greater significance. Abraham, who was called to be the father of the faithful, means 'exalted father.' Moses, who was drawn out of the Nile, literally means 'drawn out.' Samuel, the child born in answer to his mother's persistent prayers, means 'asked of the Lord.' And Jacob was actually given a new name, Israel, meaning 'a prince with God.'

One of the Old Testament names for God, Jehovah, means 'I am that I am.' The Jews held that name in such reverence that they would never read it or pronounce it. Instead, they substituted for it the more common name 'Lord.' The tradition was that only once in the year, on the Day of Atonement, was the holy name of God pronounced, and that pronouncement was made by the High Priest.

In the name of God we have the description of His essential nature as the Supreme Being. It's not that we have to add to the greatness and the holiness of God. His name is already holy. When we call for Him to hallow His name, we are asking Him to enable us to treat Him with the reverence He deserves. The bottom line is the word *reverence*. Our prayer is that He will enable us to treat Him with reverence.

A Reverent Attitude

How easy it is to take lightly the things of God. What was our attitude as we entered church last Sunday morning? 'Well, it's another Sunday. I wish I hadn't stayed out so late last night. I'm going to have a hard time staying awake through the service. I wonder if the pastor will have anything unique and interesting to say? I can't wait to get home to catch the latest in what's happening at the

Olympics. And I might just check in and see if Tiger Woods is winning the golf match.' How easy it is to slip into an accidental irreverence, whereas worship demands the highest quality attitude before God. How lightly we take the things of God when we are actually standing on holy ground. How we forfeit the privilege of even realizing we are standing on holy ground. We have the privilege of honoring the wonderful, holy name of God in the very attitude in which we worship and pray.

Reverent Conduct

The name of God is hallowed when our lives are built on a moral base that is founded in His righteousness. As followers of Jesus, as Christians, we are different. It's not a matter of how close we can come to living the way the world lives. Some of us skate on thin ice, trying to maintain our identity as Christians while living lives that are virtually indistinguishable from the nonbelievers' lifestyle. This is really a matter of discipleship. It is a matter of endeavoring to live our lives according to the Word of God.

Obedience is our standard. Those of us who are presumptuous enough to wear the label 'Christian' must expose our lives to the scrutiny of the Holy Spirit. As the old saying goes, 'If you were arrested for being a Christian, could they come up with enough evidence to convict you?' Does our conduct communicate a reverence toward God? Is His name honored, sanctified, made special by how we live?

Reverent Speech

Profanity has even made its inroad into the vocabulary of some Christians. Do we take the name of God in vain? Do we sprinkle throughout our conversations casual references to our Creator, to our Savior? His name is sacred. We bring disgrace to ourselves and to Him when we say it lightly. How often have you heard people, when they hit their thumb with a hammer, shout out 'Jesus Christ!!' How often has a missed-hit golf shot produced a 'goddamit!!!' Imagine how we would feel if every time someone made a mistake or something went wrong they cursed our names. In a way, such profanity, such blasphemy, is a kind of instinctual reverse acknowledgment of the importance of God. The persons most frequently using the name of God are often those who are the farthest from God and worship Him the least.

Check the media. How often is the name 'God' used as a term of profanity on prime time television? Whereas once it was not allowed, now it's one of the most common, casual expressions. Some time ago, the Associated Press released this statement by Rev. Donald E Wildmon, a Methodist who heads the National Federation for Decency:

> *The word God is the third most frequently used term of profanity on prime-time television, says the National Federations for Decency after monitoring 864 hours of prime-time viewing, and registering a total of 1,054 profane utterances.*

Has profanity subtly crept into our lives?

My wife Anne and I have two dogs. They are Cavalier King Charles spaniels. Originally we had just one. His name is Monty. He is a little Blenheim, and he simply adores my wife. You should see the way he follows her around the house. He holds her in reverence. About eight months after we obtained Monty, we picked up Travis, who is a Tricolor. As Monty is more attached to Anne, Travis is a bit more attached to me. He follows me around, watching my every move. These two wonderful little dogs make us both feel so special. Every analogy breaks down eventually, and this one breaks down here. We are persons created in the image of God. We can make the choice to adore Him and worship him, or not to do so. The fact is that we have the freedom as creatures to give adoration to the holy God, to honor His name, to see Him as special, to be excited about a relationship with Him, to hallow His name... or not. Just anticipating the greeting I'll receive from Monty and Travis tonight when I go home, the enthusiasm they will show, their little tails wagging like fast-moving metronomes, reminds me that the God of all creation deserves infinitely much more enthusiasm from us as we worship and adore Him.

Two men stood in Chicago's windswept Lincoln Park. One stood in awe, looking at the statue of Abraham Lincoln, 'The Great Emancipator.' Reverently he took off his hat and covered his heart with it. He had the same sense of awe of that great leader and what he stood for as many of us sensed when we saw that battered flag from Ground Zero enter the Olympic Stadium in Salt Lake City. The other man was leaning up against the pedestal on which the statue is anchored. He was writing obscenities and profanities on its base. Periodically, beyond thinking, he spit tobacco juice on the feet of Abraham Lincoln, perhaps not even aware of who Lincoln was. Has irreverence crept into our lives?

When you Pray, say… 'Your Kingdom Come.'

Jesus talked much about the Kingdom of God. It was the primary burden of His teaching.

Mark begins a narrative of our Lord's earthly ministry with these words:

> *After John was put in prison, Jesus went into Galilee, proclaiming the good news of God. 'The time has come,' He said. 'The kingdom of God is near. Repent and believe the good news!'.*

Mark 1:14

From the earliest days of His public ministry, right on through to those last moments on the cross, Jesus proclaimed the Kingdom. He invited people to enter His Kingdom. The repentant thief on the cross knew that message. He cried out:

> *'Jesus, remember me when You come into Your kingdom.' Jesus answered him, 'I tell you the truth, today you will be with me in paradise'.*

Luke 23:42-43

'Your kingdom come' calls for God to exercise His kingship. He's going to do it anyway. It's our acknowledgment that He is God and that we want Him to be sovereign. We are willing to bend our knees before Him and we are willing to take on the role of being His dedicated servants? Do we really mean that? Or are we more inclined to say, 'Let God be God and let me be God.' Or 'Let Him be sovereign in His area. Let me be sovereign in my area.' We are willing to let His kingdom come as long as it doesn't encroach on our kingdoms.

Just what is this Kingdom of God about which Jesus talks so much? There are three aspects to it.

The Kingdom of God is within us

This is what Jesus was talking about in His conversations with Nicodemus. Remember those words? 'I tell you the truth, no one can see the kingdom of God unless he is born again' (John 3:3). Nicodemus queried how a person could be born who was already a mature adult. Jesus responded, saying, 'I tell you the truth, no one can enter the kingdom of God unless he is born of water and the Spirit' (John 3:5). The Kingdom of God is within us. We become part of that kingdom as we repent of our sins and put our trust in Jesus Christ.

Our love of ease, our dread of affliction or persecution, the cares of this world, the love of riches—all these can eclipse God's kingdom work in our lives. When we talk about being converted, we actually are talking about a change in allegiance from pagan worship, which ultimately is human-centered worship, to God-centered worship. It's a shift in allegiance from self to God. It's a 180 degree turnabout in which we walk away from the kingdom of this world into the Kingdom of God. That Kingdom is within us. But our love of ease, our dread of affliction or persecution, the cares of this world, and our love of riches – all of these can eclipse God's kingdom work in our lives.

The Kingdom of God is the Visible Church, the Visible, yet Imperfect, Body of Christ on Earth. The Kingdom of God is the church, right now, here in this world. It is not a perfect church. Jesus told a story to explain it.

> *The kingdom of heaven is like a man who sowed good seed in his field. But while everyone was sleeping, his enemy came and sowed weeds among the wheat, and went away. When the wheat sprouted and formed heads, then the weeds also appeared.*
>
> *The owner's servants came to him and said, "Sir, didn't you sow good seed in your field? Where then did the weeds come from?"*
>
> *"An enemy did this," he replied.*
>
> *The servants asked him, "Do you want us to go and pull them up?"*

"No," he answered, because while you are pulling the weeds, you may root up the wheat with them. Let both grow together until the harvest. At that time I will tell the harvesters: "First collect the weeds and tie them in bundles to be burned, then gather the wheat and bring it into my barn."'

Matt. 13:24-30

The wheat represents those who are true believers, and the weeds are those who are not. The root system of the wheat is so delicate that if we went tried to root out all the weeds we would also destroy a lot of the wheat. We fail at our best efforts in trying to keep the visible church pure. We must remember this when we struggle with some of the issues that are facing our own congregations and denominations.

This is no excuse for not giving our best to this aspect of the Kingdom of God. How are you doing in this area? Are you giving your best to the church visible? Perhaps you say that you don't need the church. You have direct access to God. But the church is the gathered people of God. Too long have we allowed our 'Lone Ranger' attitude to dominate our relationship with God. We need each other. We are here together in community. When you enter church in your isolation capsule, sit for an hour-and-fifteen minutes, and then float out untouched by another human being, you have denied the Kingdom of God. Our prayer is that His Kingdom comes here on this earth to the church.

Jesus told us how we should affect the world when it looks at us as the church, his body here on earth.

Jesus said:

You are the salt of the earth. But if the salt loses its saltiness, how can it be made salty again? It is no longer good for anything, except to be thrown out and trampled by men.

You are the light of the world. A city on a hill cannot be hidden. Neither do people light a lamp and put it under a bowl. Instead they put it on its stand, and it gives light to everyone in the house. In the same way, let your light shine before men, that they may see your good deeds and praise your Father in heaven.

Matt. 5:13-16

How is your attendance? How is your devotion? Do you love the church? Are you willing to sacrifice for it? Are you willing to participate through it in making a dynamic spiritual and social impact on your community and the world? The Kingdom of God is the visible church.

*The Kingdom of God is that Full Consummation
When Jesus Christ Returns to Set all things Straight
and to Begin his Reign over all Creation.*
This is the vision of Isaiah:

> *The wolf will live with the lamb, the leopard
> will lie down with the goat, the calf and the
> lion and the yearling together; and a little
> child will lead them. The cow will feed with
> the bear, their young will lie down together,
> and the lion will ear straw like the ox. The
> infant will play near the hole of the cobra,
> and the young child put his hand into viper's
> nest. They will neither harm nor destroy in all
> my holy mountain, for the earth will be full of
> the knowledge of the Lord as the waters cover
> the sea.*
>
> Isa. 11:6-9

It is the vision of the Apostle Paul:

> *For the Lord Himself will come down from
> heaven, with a loud command, with the voice
> of the archangel and with the trumpet call of
> God, and the dead in Christ will rise first. After
> that, we who are still alive and are left will be
> caught up with them in the clouds to meet the
> Lord in the air. And so we will be with the
> Lord for ever'.*
>
> 1 Thess. 4:13-17

When the trumpet sounds, the dead in Christ will rise to meet the Triumphant King of all history. On that great day Jesus will come not on a lowly borrowed donkey, but in clouds of glory. So we cry out, 'Even so come Lord Jesus,' in our faithful anticipation of that future hope.

Are we committed to the Kingdom of God? God has placed us here to have a redemptive impact on the kingdom of humankind. We are strategically placed to be involved in friendship evangelism. We are strategically placed to give a cup of cold water in the name of Jesus Christ. Are we aware of this? Are we faithful to His call to be His ambassadors? God has chosen to work through us. Are we letting Him do it? If so, we can pray that prayer and mean it. Otherwise, we may very well be praying the prayer, 'I want my kingdom to come!'

When you Pray, say 'Your will be done.'

Do we really want the will of God? If I'm going to answer that question honestly, I have to say that I do and I don't. There are times when His will goes against my will. If I pause long enough, I realize that if I'm at all serious about my faith I really do want His will. So, I add my voice to yours, and I pray, 'Your will be done.' Then I pause and ask myself just what am I praying for?

It's one thing to pray generically for God's will to be done out there. It's another to genuinely pray for God's will to be done in and through us. Are we aware what amazing things can happen when we genuinely pray for God's will to be done in and through us? There is no limit on what is possible when we are willing to yield ourselves to the will of God, to make this our highest ambition.

God's Will is Done through us

In 1872, Dwight L. Moody attended an early morning meeting in Ireland. At that meeting, he heard a man by the name of Henry Varley say, in a quiet way, 'The world has yet to see what God can do with and for and through and in a man who is fully and wholly consecrated to Him.' The next Sunday, while listening to the great British preacher Charles Haddon Spurgeon preach, Moody's thoughts went back again to those words of Henry Varley. He said to himself, 'The world has yet to see what God can do with and for and through and in a man!' Varley meant any man! Varley didn't say he had to be educated or brilliant, or anything else - just a man! Well, by the Holy Spirit in me, I will be one of those men!'

Track the life of D. L. Moody and you'll see the impact of how God used this man who genuinely gave his life to do the will of God. He was a great evangelist, touching the hearts and lives of common men and women in the United States and in the British Isles too. He also had a quiet, gracious way with men and women powerful in business and political leadership. He taught, he preached, he founded institutions that spark-plugged higher education, ecumenical relations, and the world mission movement. God is in the business of bringing about His will through people like D. L. Moody, though people like you and me.

Although the world has only seen one Man who was wholly consecrated to God's will, that being Jesus Christ Himself who said that His calling was "to do the will of Him that sent me," there are many who have demonstrated what God can do with a man or a woman who within their own human limitations are consecrated to the will of God. I would urge you to explore the potential of what God wills through you.

God's Will is Done in us

This is a bit more difficult. Whereas our desire to see God accomplish through us lifts us to heights of leadership and altruistic service, His work in us often takes on a much less pleasant potential. It means that we are willing to expose ourselves to difficulty. It means that we are willing for Him to work in us any work He wants to work. I guarantee that will involve some pain.

That's what it meant for Joseph when his jealous brothers sold him into slavery. He wanted the will of God and he refused to do the easy thing when he resisted the sensual advances of Potiphar's wife. Prison was better than stepping out of the will of God. Those were difficult years. When he was finally elevated to a powerful position, and his identity was finally unveiled to his fearful brothers, he urged them not to be distressed or angry with themselves but acknowledged:

> *But God sent me ahead of you to preserve for you a remnant on earth and to save your lives by a great deliverance.*
>
> Gen. 45:7

That's an Old Testament version of Paul's words:

> *And we know that in all things God works for the good of those who love Him, who have been called according to His purpose.*
>
> Rom. 8:28

The highest example of dedication to the will of God was seen in Gethsemane:

> *Jesus went out as usual to the Mount of Olives,*
> *and His disciples followed him. On reaching*
> *the place, He said to them, 'Pray that you will*
> *not fall into temptation.' He withdrew about*
> *a stone's throw beyond them, knelt down and*
> *prayed, 'Father, if You are willing, take this cup*
> *from Me; yet not My will, but Yours be done.'*
> *An angel from heaven appeared to Him and*
> *strengthened Him. And being in anguish, He*
> *prayed more earnestly, and His sweat was like*
> *drops of blood falling to the ground.*
>
> Luke 22:39-45

Not only did Jesus tell His disciples how to pray for God's will to be done, but He prayed that prayer himself in His moment of greatest anguish.

Anne and I are constantly wrestling and struggling with just what God's will is for our ministry. We dare not settle in and get comfortable. We dare not enjoy the status quo. But frankly, as tough as it is to expose oneself to new dimensions of God's will for one's life, it is actually quite exciting to kneel prostrate before Him, crying out, 'Oh, God. Help me to know Your will and help me to do it.'

Just the other day I received a letter from a friend of mine who last month led a prayer workshop in his church. Getting ready for that workshop he reviewed all the prayer requests that went to his church over a period of several weeks, about 50 to 75 prayer requests per week. He writes, 'From this I concluded that 95 percent either asked for God to *give* them something, for God to *take away* something, or for God to *change* something or someone. I didn't see a single request for 'God change *me*!'

Years ago my mother gave me a magazine clipping of a poem by an unknown author. In my deepest moments of anguish, when I don't understand what God is doing in my life, I pull out this poem and read it. Then I remember that even when I don't understand the difficulty, God is working out His will in and through it.

When God wants to drill a man,
And thrill a man,
And skill a man,
When God wants to mold a man
To play the noblest part;
When He yearns with all His heart
To create so great and bold a man
That all the world shall be amazed,
Watch His methods, watch His ways!
How He ruthlessly perfects
Whom He royally elects,
How He hammers him and hurts him,
And with mighty blows converts him

Into trial shapes of clay which
Only God understands;
While his tortured heart is crying
And he lifts beseeching hands!
How He bends but never breaks
When his good He undertakes;
How He uses whom He chooses,
And with every purpose fuses him;
By every act induces him
To try His splendor out –
God knows what He's about.

I urge you to reflect upon the explosive potential of these three phrases from the Lord's Prayer that we say so quickly: 'hallowed be your name, your kingdom come, your will be done…'

Then Final Phrase, '…on earth as it is in heaven.'

We don't know much about heaven. The Bible talks about streets paved with gold. Visions are recorded of twelve pearly gates to the beautiful city. Our fantasies roam through streets filled with mansions. Then we pause and realize that these are simply God's down-to-earth terms to describe a reality that goes beyond any human description. What other facts *do* we know about heaven? It is one great empire of obedience. There God's will is gladly and perfectly done:

All the peoples of the earth are regarded as nothing. He does what He pleases with the powers of heaven and the peoples of the earth. No-one can hold back His hand or say to Him: 'What have You done?'

Dan.3:35

Heaven is the abode of God and His angels:

God is just: He will pay back trouble to those who trouble you and give relief to you who are troubled, and to us as well. This will happen when the Lord Jesus is revealed from heaven in blazing fire with his powerful angels'.

2 Thess. 1:6-7

All true believers who have died are now with God there:

For the Lord loves the just and will not forsake His faithful ones. They will be protected for ever, but the offspring of the wicked will be cut off; the righteous will inherit the land and dwell in it for ever.

Ps. 37:28

But heaven is not a place of inactivity. Christ is preparing it for His followers. Jesus said:

In my Father's house are many rooms; if it were not so, I would have told you. I am going there to prepare a place for you. And if I go and prepare a place for you, I will come back and take you to be with Me that you also may be where I am.

John 14:2-3

Jesus is also involved in intercession on our behalf before the Father:

Who will bring any charge against those whom God has chosen? It is God who justifies. Who is he that condemns? Christ Jesus, who died – more than that, who was raised to life – is at the right hand of God and is also interceding for us.

Rom. 8:33-34

In addition to these duties, Christ is preserving an eternal inheritance for us in heaven:

Praise be to the God and Father of our Lord Jesus Christ! In His great mercy He has given us new birth into a living hope through the resurrection of Jesus Christ from the dead, and into an inheritance that can never perish, spoil or fade – kept in heaven for you, who through faith are shielded by God's power until the coming of the salvation that is ready to be revealed in the last time.

1 Pet. 1:3-4

Jesus tells us to pray that God's name be hallowed, not only in heaven but on earth. Therefore Jesus tells us to pray that God's Kingdom come, not only in heaven but on earth. And it follows that Jesus tells us to pray that God's will be done, not only in heaven but on earth. Implicit in this model prayer is Jesus' instruction for you and me to get up from our knees and help Him make it happen!

Just imagine that this afternoon you get a call from the White House. The operator says, 'Just a moment, the President of the United States would like to speak with you.' I imagine that would get your attention, wouldn't it? The President then comes on the line, exchanges some friendly conversation with you, then sketches some goals he has in mind to combat terrorism. I imagine you'd listen carefully to what he has to say – even if you were of a different political persuasion! Then he calls you by name and says, 'I've a job for you to do. I need you to help me accomplish these goals. I'm going to appoint you as my ambassador at large and give you all the resources of the American government to help you further my goals.' I feel quite confident you would take him seriously, treat him with respect, and give the next era of your life, no matter what sacrifices that would entail, to help him do that job.

How can we do less than treat the God of all creation with the utmost respect and commit ourselves and our highest goals to building His Kingdom and doing His will for the rest of our lives here on earth, anticipating what it will be like in heaven!

4
Praying for Basic Necessities

'Give us today our daily bread'
(Matthew 6:11)

Jesus instructs us to pray, 'Give us today our daily bread.' This is an understandable prayer coming from an itinerant rabbi whose only possessions were His seamless garment and His sandals. How appropriate were those words to His traveling companions - men who had given up everything to follow Jesus.

Walk the streets of Calcutta, India, and these words take on tremendous meaning. Children with bloated tummies pleadingly roll their sunken eyes upward at you, their hands stretched out, begging. Or jostle along the rock-strewn dirt roadway down into Kenya's Rift Valley and into the Masai territory. View the bleaching bones of dead cattle. Approach a village only to discover people who are normally poor all the more subdued by a horrible drought. Or, in America, visit an impoverished family in any socially deprived neighborhood of any large city. Rats are the common enemy. Food is scarce, parents are jobless, and there are just too many children.

What do we say to a hungry world? What can any one of us do? Jesus urged us to pray. But prayer should not be seen as an escape from reality. We could spiritualize Christ's words and say that He was talking about spiritual bread. He did, in fact, occasionally use the idea of food in a spiritual sense. When Jesus directed his disciples to pray 'Give us today our daily bread,' was this an escape from hard reality? Was Jesus referring to some kind of spiritual bread? When He confronted Satan in that temptation anguish, having fasted for forty days and forty nights, He was being tempted to turn the stones into bread. Quoting the Scriptures, Jesus answered:

> It is written: 'Man does not live on bread alone, but on every word that comes from the mouth of God".
>
> Matt. 4:4

There is such a thing as spiritual bread.

Bread is Bread

But let's not twist the meaning of this prayer. Saints must eat; everyone must eat to stay alive. The best scholars say that it was physical bread to which Jesus was referring. And we know that Jesus was interested in providing for people's physical needs. On one occasion he fed four thousand, and on another he provided for upwards of five thousand people. He broke bread with His disciples in the Upper Room. After His journey along the Emmaus Road on the day of His resurrection, He stopped and broke bread with His two grief-stricken followers. And it is recorded that He prepared a post-resurrection meal for His disciples on the shore of the Sea of Galilee.

We can try to identify with the social and economic dynamics of His day. We can reflect on the needs of a hungry world. But does this fourth petition in the Lord's Prayer say anything to economically-stable Christians, whose next meal – and several ones following it – are already in the fridge or freezer. Although those who will read this book will come from different social classes, I doubt that there are any who are wondering how, where, or with what they will obtain today's lunch. We are physically blessed. So, since this doesn't particularly apply to us, should we just quickly move on to the next petition of what we call the Lord's Prayer? Not for a moment! The prayer is still for us, as we'll discover when we pause and savor some of the deeper teachings of this particular petition.

A Call to Humility

We are completely dependent on God. We are created in His image. We are like a high-quality bond paper. Hold it up to a lamp and you'll see a watermark. It's a sign of quality. It's an imprint that sets it aside as something special. God wants you and me to feel good about ourselves. He created us special. We are His product. We are not self-creations. Some of us pride ourselves on being self-made men and women. We've moved ahead in life. We have a list of accomplishments alongside our names. Things have gone well, and we expect them to continue going in the same direction. But we forget that every good and perfect gift comes from above.

In the mid-1970s, I pastored the First Presbyterian Church in downtown Pittsburgh, Pennsylvania. It was a great Gothic cathedral with magnificent stained-glass windows. My office on the second floor looked across a little cemetery shared by the Trinity Episcopal

Cathedral over Sixth Avenue to the Duquesne Club. That magnificent eating club, built by the Mellons and other financial tycoons, stands as a citadel of economic and industrial success. Each day, while returning phone calls, I would somewhat absentmindedly observe the comings and goings there. Successful men walked in and out of the club. Then there was a special entrance for women that took them to the one restaurant that they could share with the men. They were allowed into the rest of the club only on New Year's Day when they were given guided tours of the facility.

As I watched the top business leadership of Pittsburgh walk in and out of that club, I recognized some of them. A number had that quiet Christian grace that understood that their talents, their abilities, their human strength, their personalities, their associations, were not entirely of their own creation. The raw materials came from God. They carried themselves with humility, with the gracious acknowledgment that they were dependent upon the Lord.

Then there were those whose success had gone to their heads. In their aggressive task orientation, they had developed an enormous sense of personal pride. They had 'arrived'. They had done it all on their own and they were quite willing to take all the credit. They were like the wealthy farmer who owns several thousand acres. He's purchased the most elaborate, modern equipment. He has all the workers he needs to farm the land. He is quite content with his accomplishments. He has grown wealthy over the years, but he has forgotten several things. He forgot that no matter how hard he tried, he couldn't manufacture the soil he needed. Neither could he create the seed he needed for his crops. He still needed sun and rain, and there was no way that he could produce them on his own. But in his selfish pride, he had forgotten the daily miracles God performs (see Luke 12:16-20). There is a fine line between autonomy and dependence.

One summer we vacationed in Georgia. The rainfall for the previous four months had been almost non-existent. The eastern part of the state was parched. Corn, which should have been tall and green, was withered and brown. There wasn't much that even the most successful farmer could do about it. Even they were at the mercy of nature. In lean times this breeds humility. In affluent times it nurtures forgetfulness and pride. It doesn't take us long to forget, does it?

In America there was a gasoline crisis in the mid and late 1970s. I remember the long queues in which we sat. I remember how friendly we became with our local service station owners. When was the last time we showed him that same special attention? We will once again if there is the treat of another shortage of gasoline. When we are self-sufficient, when we don't feel the need of other people, we become proud.

Whether it be the depression of the 1930s or the recession such as we had in the early 1980s, the early 1990s, or more recently since the decline in the high-tech stocks, tough times make us humble. We realize more and more how much we need each other. In these tough times we feel, once again, our interdependence and our calling to acknowledge God's sovereignty in our lives. When we pray, 'Give us today our daily bread,' we are reminding ourselves that we need God, and we are reminding God that we are aware of this need. It is an expression of humility.

A Call to *Interpersonal Stewardship*

Jesus didn't pray, 'My Father.' Nor did He pray, 'Give me this day my daily bread.' Instead, He used the plural, personal pronouns 'us' and 'our'. Two implications arise from the use of these well-chosen words. The first has to do with our attitude toward work, and the second addresses our attitude to charity.

Our Attitude to Work

The early chapters of Genesis describe humankind's fall into sin. With it came a curse, as a result of which work ceased to be a pleasure because thorns and thistles grew up that thwarted Adam and Eve's efforts to tend God's creation. Let's remember that we were originally created to work. Although sin has brought pain into the process, Adam was working before the Fall:

> *God blessed them and God said to them, 'Be fruitful and increase in number; fill the earth and subdue it. Rule over the fish of the sea and the birds of the air and over every living creature that moves on the earth'.*
>
> Gen. 1:28

We are called to work. God doesn't lower food from the sky. He only did that temporarily during the time of the exodus.

The early church was instructed to put its able-bodied members to work. Those who refused to work were not to eat:

> *For your yourselves know how you ought to follow our example. We were not idle when we were with you, nor did we eat anyone's food without paying for it. On the contrary, we worked night and day, laboring and toiling*

so that we would not be a burden to any of you. We did this, not because we do not have the right to such help, but in order to make ourselves a model for you to follow. For even when we were with you, we gave you this rule: 'If a man will not work, he shall not eat'.

2 Thess. 3: 7-10

Having said that, Scripture instructs us to care for those who are unable to work or those for whom there are no jobs:

If anyone does not provide for his relatives, and especially for his immediate family, he has denied the faith and is worse than an unbeliever'.

1 Tim. 5:8

Jesus was not born into an effete palace existence. He was a hard worker. He worked alongside His father in the carpenter's shop. Perspiration is decorative jewelry on the brow of one who gives his energy to provide life's necessities. Some of us forget the importance of vocation. Our work is a calling. It's not just a matter of how little we can do and get by. God pity the employee who refuses to produce, the person who wants to live off of his employer. He resents the perquisites of his employer's office. This kind of worker does as little as possible, viewing his work individualistically instead of in a shared stewardship responsibility. Then there's the employer who lives off his employees. All he can think about is playing golf. He's addicted to the soft life. He fails to see the interdependence, that interpersonal stewardship.

We are in this together. We are a community of persons who live with the plural, personal pronouns. This has something to say about the type of work we do. Can a Christian, in good conscience, be involved in work that contributes to the destruction of other people's lives, whether it be in the promotion of hard liquor, the sale of illegal drugs, or the ownership of slum, residential properties? It's not mine to say what is right and what is wrong. It is my responsibility to point to the Scriptures that call for righteousness and justice. What is our attitude toward our work? Do we give it our all? Do we see it as a contribution to community life?

Our Attitude to Charity

We can't pray, 'Give us today our daily bread,' as a selfish person. The Scriptures instruct us to cast our bread upon the waters, to share with others:

Cast your bread upon the waters, for after many days you will find it again (Ecc. 11:1). Why do some Christians resent those important words which Jesus shared during His passion week? He talked about the Judgment Day. He talked about the separation of the faithful from the unfaithful as the sheep are separated from the goats. And then He said what the King will say to those on His right hand:

> *Come, you who are blessed by my Father; take your inheritance, the kingdom prepared for you since the creation of the world. For I was hungry and you gave Me something to eat, I was thirsty and you gave Me something to drink, I was a stranger and you invited Me in, I needed clothes and you clothed Me, I was sick and you looked after Me, I was in prison and you came to visit Me.*
>
> Matt. 25:34-36

Do you remember the response of the righteous? They wanted to know when Jesus had been hungry or thirsty or a stranger or naked or sick or in prison. Jesus responded by saying:

> *I tell you the truth, whatever you did for one of the least of these brothers of Mine, you did for M.*
>
> Matt. 25:40

Charity is basic to the Christian's lifestyle. Love is basic. Compassion is basic. Concern is basic. We are called to a genuine appreciation for our interpersonal relationships. That's why Communism thrived for so many decades. It thrived because the world functions like a big banquet table. There on the table is bread. Some of us, the stronger ones, grab and gorge ourselves with it, put the rest in our pockets and leave the table. All the time, there's someone else quietly pleading, politely saying, 'Please, pass the bread.' Our ears are dulled to their call. Some of us who are the most conservative, the most self-righteous, the most condemnatory against Communism, are the very ones who produced it. For when people get hungry enough they are willing to trade their freedom for a loaf of bread. Survival at any price is the desperate person's willing accommodation. When Jesus prays, 'Give us today our daily bread,' He is calling you and me to an interpersonal stewardship that looks beyond our selfish concerns to see both our responsibility to work hard and to share the fruits of our labor.

A Call to *Moderation*

I would just as soon not have to write about this point, as I know I still have some lessons to learn in this area of my life. Bread literally means the basic necessities. Jesus is talking about clothing, shelter, food, and every basic material need. He has never promised us that He will meet our extravagant demands. We want more and more. The more we get the more we want. The more we want and the more we get, the more we become enslaved by what we have. Ralph Waldo Emerson stated it so succinctly, 'My household suffers from too many servants. My cows milk me.' Although we have no servants and no cows, our possessions do dominate. Our closets are filled. Instead of reducing what we have, we add more. Many of these extra things we have are good things. But are they necessary?

Perhaps we ought to read again and again, the children's tale of *Gulliver's Travels*. Remember the shipwrecked Gulliver was set upon in his slumber by the tiny Lilliputans who bound him with hundreds of ropes? Those ropes were only the thinnest of threads and yet by the very multitude of them he was bound. He could have broken each one of them, or even several of them, with no difficulty at all. But there was no way he could break himself free from the hundreds of threads with which they bound him. Are we tightly bound by the threads of our accumulated material possessions? Are we bound by the multiplicity of things that we consider essential to our existence, but which in reality are dispensable?

How we quest after money, though there is no way we can eat dollar bills. Remember King Midas? He longed, above all else, to have the power of turning everything he touched into gold. When that power was granted, he went about his palace touching this and that. His wealth was piling up by the millions. Then he grew hungry. He reached for his bread. It turned to gold. The water became gold to the touch of his thirsty lips. He found that all his wealth amounted to nothing for he could neither eat for drink. Many people who own several homes admit they are on a treadmill as they try to keep them up. They can't really enjoy any one of their homes, because the reality is that they don't own their properties, their properties own them.

The spirit of moderation doesn't come easily. As someone has said, we spend the first part of our lives accumulating things and the last part of our lives getting rid of them.

I remember when some dear friends of mine simply began to give away all their worldly possessions. He had been a professor for many years. They had some beautiful material goods. Then they got rid of them. I'll never forget him describing his newfound freedom. His things no longer enslaved him.

When Jesus teaches us, 'Give us today our daily bread,' He is urging us to pray for essentials. We are called to pray for basics. There is no promise that He will uphold our extravagant lifestyles.

A Call to Simply *Trust God*

Scholars debate what is meant by our 'daily bread'. The Greek word used here appears nowhere else in the New Testament except in Luke's version of the prayer. And it appears nowhere else in Greek non-Christian writings except for one papyrus. This is a leaf from a cook's household account. And the elusive word comes in an entry under the fifteenth day, apparently in relation to a semi-monthly reckoning. This solitary reference seems to support the translation 'daily' or 'every day' bread. Scholars suggest several possible derivations for the word. The four that are most likely are: necessary bread, dependable bread, daily bread and bread for the morrow.

The whole emphasis here is that we are called to trust God for our immediate provision. We have that exodus experience that models for us the Christian lifestyle. Remember how the manna was provided on a daily basis, six days a week? They gathered just enough for that day. On the sixth day, they gathered double the amount so they would not have to work on the Sabbath. If they tried to gather more than the immediate provision, the stuff spoiled. It turned to corruption. Have you ever tried to eat one meal that would last forever? At times some of us look as if we are trying to do just that. There's no way that we can eat enough for 365 days, much less a lifetime. Bread does not keep. It ultimately gets moldy and spoils. Jesus urges us to pray for what we need. He urges us to trust God for that which is justly ours.

Let me give you a personal example. Although I'm not basically a worrier, there are some things that I have a difficult time trusting to God. I worried about educating our children. I watched as college costs grew higher and higher every year. Although I was well paid and I had no economic worries of an immediate nature, I projected those worries out into the future. I got all shook up wondering how we would ever be able to educate our three daughters. In fact, I obsessed on it, allowing it to spoil my peace of mind while I watched some kids whose parents had more than enough money show no interest in higher education. And I watched some children whose parents have a lot less than I had work together as a family to provide top-quality education that, through mutual sacrifice, became a deeply appreciated reality. Now I look back and realize that God, in extraordinary ways, provided. And our children have their educations.

Now I can obsess about having adequate provision for retirement. Longevity seems to be in Anne's and my genes. Both sets of our parents lived into their nineties. Since I am now in my mid-sixties, I could get all worried, if I allowed myself, about issues of finance and health, allowing those fears to ruin the very life God has given me to live right now.

I remember in the early 1980s, when we were embarking on a major building program in which we built and/or remodeled our present church complex, I worried about buying the last two houses on the street. I obsessed over whether or not we would get neighbors to agree to our plans, and whether the city council would give its approval. Then, where would all the money come from? I literally ground my teeth night after night. I look back and realize we burned the mortgage documentation almost a decade ago. Now I can worry about the 'Building the Future' capital program. Once again, I want this to be something that will be a positive for our neighbors, not a negative. How can we best modify our plans to provide the Youth/Family Center, more adequate parking, the remodeling that's appropriate, and the purchase of additional land? Will we have enough money? And so it could go on.

Jesus cuts through all of our self-centered preoccupation with the present and the future by adding some fascinating comments to the Lord's Prayer. He warns us against laying up for ourselves treasures on earth where moth and rust consume and thieves break in and steal. He urges us to trust Him and make our major investment in eternal matters. He urges us not to be anxious about life, about food, about drink, about clothing. Instead, He urges us to look at the birds and how God takes care of them. The Lord reminds us that all the worry in the world can't add even as much as one more inch to one's height or one more day to one's life. Why worry about clothing? The lilies are well adorned. He concludes:

So do not worry, saying, 'What shall we eat?' or 'What shall we drink?' or 'What shall we wear?' For the pagans run after all these things, and your heavenly Father knows that you need them. But seek first His kingdom and His righteousness, and all these things will be given to you as well. Therefore do not worry about tomorrow, for tomorrow will worry about itself. Each day has enough trouble of its own.

Matt. 6:31-34

When Jesus says, 'Give us today our daily bread,' He is urging us to simply trust God! Please know that I'm not being cavalier as I uphold these teachings of God's Word. We as Christians have never been promised that our lives will be easy. But we have been told to trust God. I've discovered His faithfulness is validated the longer I live. Yet the longer I live the more I'm aware of the pain and tragedy in this world.

One Day at a Time

Some time ago, Anne and I, along with some friends in World Vision, visited Ground Zero in New York City. As we stood on the platform, looking down at that tragic site, what we saw looked more like the excavation for a new building project. But then, as we looked at the surrounding buildings, we saw the clear evidences of those tragic 9/11 events.

Together, we wandered through St Paul's Church where simultaneously worship was being held in the center part of the sanctuary while all around the internal perimeter of the sanctuary were kids stretched out on cots catching a nap or being given sandwiches or having their medical needs seen to. The walls of that church were covered with thousands of messages from all over the world. And mementoes from various fire departments, police departments, schools and cities, covered every bit of space available. We could not help but identify with those thousands of persons whose lives were so quickly and so arbitrarily lost by that horrendous act of terrorism. We could not help but think of adults left widowed and children orphaned.

Jesus himself raised questions as to who is at fault when the tragedies of life hit home? Why is a person born blind? Why does a tower fall on innocent workers and bystanders? Why does one person's test come back with bad news of malignancy? Why does another come back with the good news that for now they've dodged the bullet? And Jesus wept over the city of Jerusalem.

Tragedies cause me to come to grips with the profound teaching Jesus gave at the end of Matthew 6:34. He tells us straightforwardly that there will be trouble in this world. We should expect it, not be surprised by it. He says:

> *Therefore do not worry about tomorrow, for tomorrow will worry about itself. Each day has enough trouble of its own.*

I've discovered the truth of what Jesus said. I've worried about possible future trouble that never happen, only to be surprised by something I never thought to worry about. Today's realities are enough trouble to handle with God's help.

I find myself resonating with godly persons who help me handle grief over the tragedies and losses that happen and are beyond my explanation, even as I try to trust God for His help in present difficulties as well as the uncertain future. Gregory of Nyssa stated it so well in his *De Beatitudine*, 'It is impossible for one to live without tears who considers things exactly as they are.' Max Lucado more recently wrote, in *No Wonder They Call Him Savior*, 'The principle is simple: when words are most empty, tears are most apt.'

Jesus calls us to humility, to interpersonal stewardship, to moderation, to a simple trust in God, a trust that is adequate for this life and the next. May God enrich our understanding of the huge issues raised by a simple prayer for the provision of our daily bread.

5

Forgiven and Forgiving

'Forgive us our debts,
as we also have forgiven our debtors'
(Matt. 6:12)

Every time I visit the Middle East, traveling through Egypt, Israel, Turkey, Greece and Italy, I am overwhelmed by the radical nature of the gospel of Jesus Christ and its revolutionary impact on humankind. The first-century 'coin of the realm' was the same as that of our twenty-first century. It was power - the capacity to intimidate by military, economic and psychological strength. The 'coin of the realm' in the kingdom of God differs from that of this world. Jesus introduced a radical new way of doing business. His was a new language that talked of peace with God and with each other. He introduced a new language and lifestyle.

Forgiveness is both the language and the lifestyle of heaven. It is the coin Heaven is a world free from hostility. Recrimination will have no place there. The lion and lamb will lie down together. It will be a place marked by perfect peace. Even though forgiveness is the language and lifestyle of heaven, we don't wait until we get there to learn it. It must be learned here on earth. Forgiveness is part of this life. That's why Jesus taught us to pray, 'Forgive us our debts, as we also have forgiven our debtors' (Matt. 6:12). With these timely words, Jesus is making two key assertions that apply to each one of us. He offers to radicalize us and our lives into a whole new way of doing business as He teaches us the importance of being *forgiven* and being *forgiving*.

The Need for Forgiveness

Before we can honestly pray the Lord's Prayer, we need to be convinced of our need for continuing forgiveness. We need to be *forgiven*. There is a prayer within the Lord's Prayer that, if not prayed with sincerity, will render all the rest of our praying vain. We are in constant need of God's forgiveness. Granted, we have His imputed righteousness. We are made holy by Him, so much so, that Scripture tells us that when we meet Him we will be like Jesus!

No matter how we may define our terminology, in the final analysis, we are still saved by God's grace, and by God's grace alone. We may be clothed in His righteousness, but we still have that bent toward sin. We still need His continual cleansing. We still need to cry out with the Psalmist:

> Create in me a clean heart, O God, and renew
> a steadfast spirit within me.
>
> Ps. 51:10

This prayer, 'Forgive us our debts... ,' takes for granted that we admit that we are sinners. That presupposition undergirds the entire Lord's Prayer. No number of rationalizations on our part exempt us from being sinners.

The word 'debts', used by us Presbyterians, can muddy the waters. Seldom do I have a wedding or a funeral in which I lead the congregation in the Lord's Prayer but that we come to that awkward point where prayer moves from the vertical to the horizontal as each of us tunes our ears to hear whether the majority will mumble 'debts' or 'trespasses' so that we can quickly follow the crowd.

While the word 'debts' sounds mercantile, the word 'trespasses' evokes pictures of someone illegally walking on someone else's property. I don't think it is an accident that we Presbyterians, who have historically been the mercantile class, use the word 'debts'. We tend to define ourselves by a balance sheet. The Episcopalians, who were historically the landed gentry, probably feel more comfortable with the term 'trespasses' and those who 'trespass against us'.

Jesus uses three different words for sin.

The first of these words is the Greek word *opheilemata*. This word means debts. It is the word used by Matthew as he puts into Greek writing the oral Aramaic teachings of Jesus. This word 'debt' means a failure to pay that which is due. It's a failure in duty. It's not simply an economic shortfall. Each of us is involved in this failure. Not one of us can claim that he has perfectly fulfilled his duty to his fellow human beings and to God. There is no such perfection in this life. The sooner we realize that the better off we'll be.

The second of these words is *paraptomata*. Jesus uses this word two verses later when He talks about us forgiving others their trespasses. He says:

For if you forgive men when they sin against you, your heavenly Father will also forgive you. But if you do not forgive men their sins, your Father will not forgive your sins.

Matt. 6:14-15

This word carries the idea of illegally stepping over a boundary line. It implies a slipping and sliding process in which our lives go out of control just as a car would go out of control on an icy road. It's not a deliberate sinning. It's simply a case of being swept away by some impulse or some momentary passion that grabs control of our lives and makes us lose our self-control. The very strongest of us can slip into sin. Even the most mature Christian can get caught off guard morally and end up looking like the distinguished gentleman dressed up in evening clothes whose fine patent leather shoes touch an icy patch and, the next thing he knows, he is sprawled out in a snow bank.

There's a third word. This one is used by Luke as he puts the Lord's Prayer into writing in Luke 11:4. This word is *hamartia*, and it means sins. That is how it is translated in King James Version, the Revised Standard Version, and the New International Version. Once again, remember that Jesus did His teaching in Aramaic. The synoptic gospel writers had to translate His words into Greek. So Luke chose this word for sin. This word was originally a word referring to archery, and it literally means 'a missing of the target.' Therefore, sin is the failure to be what we might be and could be. It's a failure to live up to the promise. It's the realization that we have not turned out to be as good a husband or as good a wife as we would like to be. We're not the son or daughter we could have been. We've not lived up to our promise in terms of our life career. Sin means the failure to hit the target. We've fallen short of the bull's eye. That's what the Apostle Paul is getting at when, in Romans 3:23, he declares, 'for all have sinned and fall short of the glory of God...' None of us is exempt from sin. The Westminster Shorter Catechism brings these various understandings of sin into this one, straightforward definition: 'Sin is any want of conformity to, or transgression of, the law of God.' So we can see sin in its varied dimensions.

Sin is Doing what we Know is Wrong

It is *active* in nature. We call these sins of 'commission.' It's the choice of the lower rather than the higher. Is there one of us who has not purposely done things we know we should not have done? Visit various holocaust museums throughout the world. The world, our world, watched that horrendous annihilation of almost six million Jews. That did not happen in the Middle Ages. This happened within the lifetime of many of us. Whatever may have been the rationalizations of the Nazi leaders, they set out to do what was wrong. They destroyed God-given life. In our own much more subtle ways, we hurt others. We destroy what God has created. We wreak havoc on others and ourselves in our act of rebellion.

Sin Also is a Failure to do what we Know is Right
It is *passive* in nature. We call these sins of 'omission'. The Bible says, 'To him that knoweth to do good and doeth it not, to him it is sin' (James 4:17 AV). The priest and the Levite who walked by the man injured on the road to Jericho were guilty of sins of omission. They could have stopped, but they didn't. They rationalized that they had something more important to do. The churches in Nazi Germany, that closed their eyes to those atrocities, bear a responsibility for sins of omission. And each of us today also bears responsibilities for our failure to live up to the high standard that God has set for us. We have left undone some things we should have done.

Sin is Being Less than we were Created to Be
This was Samson's problem when he broke his Nazarite vows. It was not that he was worse than other people. It simply was that he became like other people. He failed to live up to God's standard for his life. Some of us are not actively engaged in rebellion against God. Some of us are not passively refusing to do the things that He wants us to do. Some of us are simply settling in to commonplace living, unwilling to attain the high standard that is His for us.

From time to time I look at myself and my ministry and I discover myself not to be as loving as I could and should be. I'm beginning to learn some lessons as I feel my own heart broken and observe myself breaking the hearts of others by my indifference, my insensitivity, and my selfishness. More and more I see my own bent toward elitism, my own pride of where I've been, what I've done, and what I've accomplished. How embarrassing it is to realize the superficiality of my very standards of measurement. The Lord's Prayer puts a mirror in front of us. We see ourselves as sinners: not all bad, but certainly not all good. All sin, whatever its type and whatever its origin, must either be punished or forgiven. That is a reality we must never forget.

Forgiven

In many of our worship services we recite the Apostle's Creed. Are we aware of what we are saying when we recite it? We are saying, 'I believe in the forgiveness of sins.' What a triumphant affirmation! This underlines our need for confession. At the Day of Judgment we will either stand condemned and be sent to eternal punishment for our sins or, if we have confessed our sins, we will stand forgiven. Forgiveness is based on the cross of Jesus Christ. The Bible assures us that He puts our sins as far away from us as the East is from the West.

This is not just an academic prayer. We have to pray it with the conviction of need. No matter how religious we are, our prayer is that of the publican, 'God, be merciful to me, a sinner' (Luke 18:13). The ironic thing is that the true saints of history are not persons who are aware of their self-righteousness and good works. The true saints are all the more aware of sin and their need of the Savior, their need of pardon.

More than simple pardon, forgiveness involves reconciliation. Some years ago, back in the days when there was the frequent use of capital punishment in the state of Tennessee, I was privileged to talk with the Governor of that state. His name was Frank Clement. He shared with two or three of us the awful pain he went through when he had to make decisions as to who would be pardoned and who would die. From his perspective, each of these persons was guilty. To use his privilege of pardon seemed so arbitrary.

All of us are guilty, are we not? Every one of us is worthy of punishment for sin that breaks the heart of God. Each of us needs His pardon, not a pardon that diminishes the seriousness of our offense, but one that offers us His unmerited grace that forgives us and reconciles us to Himself. I am reminded of the defense lawyer who was pleading his client's case in a jury trial. With great eloquence the lawyer swayed the jury and it returned a Not Guilty verdict. Immediately the defendant rushed up to his lawyer with profuse expressions of gratitude. Coldly, the lawyer responded, 'Off with you. You are as guilty as hell!' God could, like the lawyer, have used his prerogative to plead our case, provide remission and declare us pardoned, yet not want anything to do with us in the future. But instead, God reconciles us through His Son and embraces us to Himself as His forgiven children.

We are called to pray for forgiveness. And this forgiveness involves reconciliation, restoration. The trust relationship between us and our God was not cheaply purchased. It's nothing to take lightly. When we pray the Lord's Prayer, we pray for forgiveness.

Forgiving

Before we can honestly pray the Lord's Prayer, we must not only be aware of our need to be forgiven, we must also be mindful of our need to be *forgiving*. Some of us are pretty good at asking for forgiveness for ourselves. We're not so good at forgiving others. The Bible makes it clear that there are some conditions that must be met by us if we are to be forgiven. What are those conditions? One is the condition of *repentance*. Another condition of forgiveness is *faith in Jesus Christ*. We are called to trust Him and His provision for us. Jesus adds the third condition when He says, 'Forgive us our debts as we also have forgiven our debtors.' This is the only portion of the Lord's Prayer on which He elaborated. As we've already seen, He goes on to say:

> *For if you forgive men when they sin against you, your heavenly Father will also forgive you. But if you do not forgive men their sins, your Father will not forgive your sins.*

Matt. 6:14-15

Jesus is calling us to a forgiving attitude toward others. We can't, however, purchase our forgiveness by forgiving others. Being forgiving is a condition of forgiveness. Our forgiveness from Jesus Christ is not based on our merit. It doesn't mean that God forgives only in equal measure as we are willing to forgive. We don't create the grounds of our forgiveness. But it does create the grounds on which we are free to receive it.

If an unforgiving spirit clutters our lives, there's no way we can receive freely His forgiveness directed toward us. The Apostle Paul reminds us:

> *Be kind and compassionate to one another, forgiving each other, just as in Christ God forgave you.*
>
> Eph. 4:38

Jesus models what it is to have a forgiving spirit. We can't really pray the Lord's Prayer if we are unwilling to forgive. Jesus teaches us to ask God to forgive *us* as *we* forgive others.

Again, plural pronouns drive home the point that we are a people who live in community. We are not solitary individuals who are getting right with God. We are persons who are related to God. As He gives us His forgiveness, we are responsible for giving the same forgiveness to others, no matter what they have done to us. There is no way that we can nurse hatred and resentment while praying this prayer with authenticity. Otherwise we're praying, 'God, forgive this person that I myself won't forgive.' What we're really saying is, 'I'll never forgive, God. But you go ahead, and you forgive.'

When the great Scottish writer, Robert Louis Stevenson, lived in the South Sea Islands, he used to conduct family worship each morning. It always concluded with the Lord's Prayer. One morning, in the middle of the Lord's Prayer, Stevenson rose from his knees and left the room. As his health was always somewhat precarious, his wife followed him out of the room, thinking that he was ill. She asked, 'Is there anything wrong?' He responded, 'Only this. I'm not fit to pray the Lord's Prayer today.' We are not fit to pray the Lord's Prayer if an unforgiving spirit holds our heart in its clutches. If we have not put things right with others, we cannot get things right with God. Not only that, the most miserable person in the world is the one who won't forgive. Nothing gnarls a soul more quickly. It has been said so aptly, 'If I had an enemy whom I wanted to punish, I would teach him to hate someone.'

Being truly forgiven makes us much more willing to forgive others. If we think our sins are forgiven, and we refuse to forgive somebody else, we make a mistake, the mistake of thinking that our sins have been forgiven when they have not. We all need to search our hearts to see if we are harboring cases of unforgiveness there. As I considered this material, I reviewed my whole life to check for any unforgiveness in me. Then I listed people whom I felt had wronged me. Afterward, I ripped that list apart and let go of my resentments. I asked God's forgiveness for my unwillingness to forgive. Perhaps all of us need to make similar lists. Can we let go? Can we forgive? Are we willing both to forgive and be forgiven?

I have seen leaders of Divorce Recovery Workshops help men and women, embittered by the unfairness of divorce, learn to forgive the ones who wronged them. It's not easy to do, but the alternative is being a slave to an unforgiving spirit. In that way, we let the other person have complete control over us, destroying us a second time. How much better to be liberated from that destructive control and help that other person get a fresh start in life.

The Story of Two Debtors

One day Jesus told a story about a king. This king was getting his accounts straightened out with his servants. One poor fellow was brought before him who had become hopelessly indebted to the king. He owed the equivalent of millions of dollars. He didn't have a penny with which to pay his debt. The king, not willing to lose all his money, ordered the man to be sold into slavery, along with his wife and children. What a sad set of circumstances.

The poor fellow, when he realized that his debt meant ruin, not only to himself but to those he loved, fell on his face before the king and pleaded for time. He begged for patience. 'Give me time, and I'll pay you back everything I owe you!' The king, out of pure kindness, did far more. Touched by this poor man's plight, he canceled the entire debt and sent him away a free man. What a difference. The former debtor's eyes sparkled and his face was bright. His stooped shoulders were squared and he walked tall. Had you asked him, 'What in the world has happened?' He would have told you his story. 'An hour ago, I was hopelessly in debt. I didn't have a penny to pay the king the money I owed him. He was ready to sell me, and my wife and children, into slavery just to get some of the money back. I begged for a little time to settle my enormous debt. Do you know what his Majesty did? He canceled the debt all together!'

If you had met the same man a short while later, you would have seen a terrible difference in his appearance. The light and excitement had gone from his eyes. His face had become hardened and sullen. You wonder what caused this terrible change. But all becomes clear when you see him reach out and seize a shabbily dressed man by the collar, and snarl at him, 'Pay me that $50 you owe me!' The poor fellow flings himself down, prays the same prayer his harsh creditor had prayed to the king. But his plea is in vain. The face that bent above him did not soften. Instead it became harder and more cruel as his creditor casts him into prison.

You know the rest of the story. The king summoned the forgiven servant. He confronted him with the tragic inconsistency and reminded him of the forgiveness given which should have challenged him to show mercy on another. Angrily, the king re-arrests him and delivers him to the jailers.

'You wicked servant,' he said, 'I canceled all that debt of yours because you begged me to. Shouldn't you have had mercy on your fellow servant just as I had on you?' In anger his master turned him over to the jailers until he should pay back all he owed.

'This,' says Jesus, 'is how my heavenly Father will treat each one of you unless you forgive your brother from your heart'.

Matt. 18:32-35

In the book *Quo Vadis*, the wicked Chilo had sold the wife and daughter of his friend Glaucus into slavery and tried to kill him for his faith in Jesus Christ. Glaucus was one of those Christians, each of whom was covered with pitch, fastened to a pillar, and then set on fire in the Roman gardens for the amusement of Nero. As Nero and Chilo reviewed the human tortures, they came to the pillar where Glaucus was burning, still alive and conscious. The wind blew the smoke away for a moment, disclosing the face of Glaucus. Chilo was seized with a sudden sense of conscience and bitter remorse. Stretching his arms up toward the agonized martyr he cried out, 'Glaucus, in Christ's name, forgive me!' At that, the head of the martyr moved slightly and, from the top of the pillar, was heard the voice of Glaucus, like a groan, 'I forgive.'

A strange light came into the face of Chilo. Turning toward Nero and lifting an accusing finger, he cried out, 'There is the incendiary!' In the excitement that followed, Chilo encountered St Paul in the crowd, and Paul told him of the infinite forgiveness of Jesus Christ. Chilo was baptized into the faith. The next day, when Chilo himself was in the hands of Nero's torturers who demanded that he retract his Christian confession, he asked that he might die as the other Christians died. When his torturers are binding him with ropes and piercing him with iron tongs, Chilo humbly kissed their hands and forgave them. Forgiven himself, he had learned to forgive. And he died a man at peace!

The questions we all have to ask ourselves are these: are we forgiven? and are we willing to forgive?

6

Praying About Temptation

'And lead us not into temptation
but deliver us from the evil one'.
Matt 6:13

When Jesus teaches His disciples to pray, 'And lead us not into temptation…' is He implying that God purposely leads His children into temptation? At first glance, the answer seems to be 'yes'. But our minds immediately recall the writing of James who stated:

When tempted, no one should say, 'God is tempting me.' For God cannot be tempted by evil, nor does He tempt anyone; but each one is tempted when, by his own evil desire, he is dragged away and enticed.

James 1:13-14

First we need to *understand* what appears to be biblical confusion. Then we need to *apply* the teachings of Jesus about temptation to our own daily lives.

Temptation as an Inducement to Evil

Temptation has two primary meanings. It can mean *inducement to evil.* It is the pressure that is brought about by Satan who encourages us to disobey God. Temptation is a spiritual-moral seduction. But God never invites us down the low road. It is not His will that we sin. In no way is God evil. Nor is He a God who inclines us toward evil. God is a good God, a righteous God, who yearns to have us live according to His righteous standards. At the same time, God allows us to be tempted. He has given us the capacity to choose between right and wrong. We have the choice to go His way in obedience, or we can disobey.

Adam and Eve, the highest of all God's creation, were placed in the beautiful garden. They were given the responsibility to tend the Garden of Eden. There was only one prohibition. God commanded, 'You are free to eat from any tree in the garden; but you must not eat from the tree of the knowledge of good and evil, for when you eat of it you will surely die' (Gen. 2:16-17). Along came the seducer, Satan in the form of a serpent. False promises were made. The freedom of choice was carried out. Eve, then Adam, ate the fruit of the forbidden tree. Their eyes were opened. They saw each other's nakedness in a whole new light. What once represented health, wholeness and openness of communication, became distorted. Feeling exposed, they sewed fig leaves together and made themselves aprons. Then they heard the sound of the Lord walking in the garden in the cool of the day. Adam and Eve hid themselves from the presence of the Lord, only to discover the omnipresence and omniscience of the sovereign God who had refused to create a mechanical man or a mechanical woman who would be nothing more than worship machines.

God gives freedom. Temptation is a fact of our existence. God allows it. Matthew states, 'Then Jesus was led by the Spirit into the desert to be tempted by the devil' (Matt. 4:1). So we see that although God is not the tempter, He does allow the tempter to do his business. Although God is a righteous God, we have the freedom to disobey Him. We are free to sin.

And we are free to reap the results of our sin.

Jesus instructs us to pray, 'And lead us not into temptation, but deliver us from the evil one.' That's the prayer to pray early in the morning as we face a new day. Each day we walk into a world that is full of evil. Temptation after temptation will come our way.

Dr Clarence Macartney, the great preacher of the First Presbyterian Church of Pittsburgh in the early part of the last century, put it in these words:

> In every circumstance of life, every lot, every association, every labor, every pleasure or hardship, there is a possible temptation. There are temptations for the body, for the mind, for the soul. There are the temptations to the appetite, to selfishness, dishonesty, to the evasion of duty, the disregard of others' rights, indifference to others' sorrows; pride, sloth, envy, suspicion, taking up an evil report against our neighbor, and the subtle, but even more dangerous, temptations to doubt, to unbelief. What a world it is, with Satan desiring to have us that he may sift us as wheat! Hence, how earnestly we ought to make this prayer, 'Lead us not into temptation, but deliver us from evil.'

In this petition, Jesus teaches us how to enter a dangerous world and how to pass through it in safety.

Temptation as a Test or Trial

God never leads us into any situation unless it has the potential for good. The problem is that most situations that have a potential for good also have a potential for evil. The Lord is not the author of evil; He does not want us to sin. However, every person needs to be tested. There is great value in the testing process. For example, the laws of aerodynamics demand that a new wing structure be tested before it is used on a commercial aircraft. Scientists know its stress factors. They don't want to risk innocent lives to metal fatigue. Likewise, every Christian goes through the valuable process of testing. God allows us to be tested and tried because we are strengthened through tough experiences.

Think of the godly Job. His pleasant friends tried to answer the unanswerable question of why a just man should suffer. How hollow were their well-intentioned remarks. And they were absolutely wrong in their thinking. In fact, most of our endeavors to explain how a good God can allow what appears to be evil leave us with more questions than answers. Then we see the ups and downs in Israel's fortunes. Some of the downs can be attributed to sin, but not all. History is filled with innocent sufferers. Jesus made reference to those people who were killed when a tower fell over. He didn't explain why, but He did attack the wrong answer that some were inclined to give.

Life has its troubles. Difficulties mark our existence. All trouble tests our moral, spiritual and emotional fiber. Testing has its value and even tragedy can bring out the best in us.

The Apostle Paul put it in these words:

> … we rejoice in the hope of the glory of God. Not only so, but we also rejoice in our sufferings, because we know that suffering produces perseverance; perseverance, character; and character, hope. And hope does not disappoint us, because God has poured out His love into our hearts by the Holy Spirit, whom He has given us.
>
> Rom. 5:3-5

James adds to the words of Paul. He writes:

> Consider it pure joy, my brothers, whenever you face trials of many kinds, because you know that the testing of your faith develops perseverance. Perseverance must finish its work so that you may be mature and complete, not lacking anything.
>
> James 1:2-4

There is a warning implied in God's Word. God can test us, but we are not to test Him. We are to trust Him. Ours is not the business of daring God. He has given His promises and we are to rely on them, which does not mean that we are to cast ourselves into dangerous situations just to see how the Lord delivers us out of them. There are some who would handle poisonous snakes in the name of Jesus Christ. But while God could certainly protect them, they are fools to play such a game to try to evoke a demonstration of God's power.

Jesus refused to tempt God. When He was led up to the pinnacle of the Temple, Satan dared Him to jump. I've stood at that high spot, looking deep down into the valley below. It is a frightening plunge from the high corner wall of the temple area in Jerusalem. Satan dared Jesus, taunting the Lord with his claim to be the Son of God. The devil challenged Jesus to throw Himself down, reminding Him that God's angels would take care of Him. Jesus responded, quoting the Scripture, 'Do not put the Lord your God to the test,' words with which the Lord was familiar from Deuteronomy.

Do not test the Lord your God as you did at Massah.

Deut. 6:16

Seduction or Testing?

So we see, the temptation has two meanings. It is both a satanic inducement to evil and a test or trial. As Christians, we face both kinds of temptation. But understanding the meanings of the word temptation does not total clear the confusion. We could say that if the word means seduction, the prayer is unnecessary because God does not seduce. And if the word means testing, the prayer seems unworthy. We ought not to shrink from testing.

In fact, both meanings are present. And here we have one of the most exciting facts of God's understanding. It is this: Jesus understands us. He is teaching us how to pray with a conscious sense of our human weakness. He is not teaching us how to pray as an exercise in logic. A logician demands terms precisely defined. I'm afraid that we have needs that go far beyond precise definition. Jesus knows those needs. He is teaching us how to pray the outcry of the soul in need. Isn't Jesus magnificent in the way He helps us articulate our deepest needs, however fixed our motives may be? Our prayer is that God will not lead us into temptation - either that which will produce moral failure or that which will put such pressure on us that it will break us, rendering us useless in his service!

This prayer is the prayer of a forgiven and forgiving person who wants a continuing right relationship with God. The one who prays this prayer is not presuming on God by thinking he is ready to undergo any temptation. He is not saying, 'Lord, lead me into any kind of temptation because I am strong enough to bear it.' Instead he is saying, 'Lord, don't lead me into temptation lest I'm not strong enough to bear it.' God knows when we are ready to be tested, and won't test us when we are not strong enough:

> God is faithful; He will not let you be tempted beyond what you can bear. But when you are tempted, He will also provide a way out so that you can stand up under it.
>
> 1 Cor. 10:13

Note what follows. Jesus has taught us to ask for God's forgiveness even as we forgive others who need our forgiveness. Those of us who are presumptuous enough to ask for His help in the area of temptation are persons who have some overwhelming convictions.

The Deadly Nature of Sin

There are many kinds of fears. Some of us are afraid of heights, others are afraid of being alone.

Some are afraid of being locked in an elevator, being closed in a confined space with other people. Some are afraid of germs, and others fear death. Anne and I, early in our marriage, lived in an apartment building. Across the street there was a high-rise apartment. We were told about a man who lived there who was so fearful of germs that he tried to live an antiseptic existence. He wore sterilized gloves. He made everyone coming into his apartment take off their shoes. If you picked up his phone, you had to cradle it in a tissue that was immediately thrown away when you were finished. He sprayed everything with antiseptic. He was scared to death of germs that he tried to live an antiseptic life.

We smile when we hear about such a person. Some people's phobias amuse us. But there is nothing funny about the fear of sin. Sin is malignant. Just as cancer is a growth, so is sin. It takes over. It eats away at the vitals of our spiritual existence. It makes us terminally ill. James underlines sin's downward spiraling effect:

> ... each of us in tempted when, by his own evil desire, he is dragged away and enticed. Then, after desire has conceived, it gives birth to sin; and sin, when it is full-grown, gives birth to death.

> James 1:14-15

So we are forced to put the question to ourselves. What do I read? What is my thought life like? What are those precious, private thoughts toward God, myself, other people? Jesus put it like this:

> For out of the heart come evil thoughts, murder, adultery, sexual immorality, theft, false testimony, slander'.
>
> Matt. 15:19

We have all heard of people, some of them very high profile, who tried to take the easy way up the professional ladder by falsifying their qualifications, giving themselves degrees they didn't study for and doctorates they were never awarded. These people discover the downward spiral of evil, for their initial lie leads to so many lies that they must be in danger of forgetting the truth. Then when they are discovered to have lied, their downfall is often both public and long lasting, as few employers would ever be prepared to trust them again.

Although the movie, 'Unfaithful' showed some fairly explicit scenes, it could be described as a modern morality tale that shows vividly the terrible consequences of adultery. a suburban housewife and mother struggled with her conscience as she gradually moved into an affair. Initially reluctant, then consumed by her romantic feelings combined with lust, her experience spiraled downward to guilt and remorse. By the time she finally tried to break off the relationship, it was too late. She had destroyed her life and the lives of her husband, her son and even her lover.

When we pray about temptation we mean business. It's the cry of a soul yearning for righteousness because it knows the deadly nature of sin.

Our Own Weakness

Because we are always in danger of becoming over-confident, praying against that should be part of our daily devotions. We are called to be humble before God, and that should remind us also to be humble before men. How often have we seen an athletic team beaten because it was over confident? You may also have seen a speaker lose what he was saying because he was over confident. And I have to confess that speaker might have been me. I was once presiding at a wedding and I had four little comments to make in the way of a meditation. They were highly personal words directed to the bride and groom. I announced that I wanted to share four challenges. They were points that I had thought through on another occasion, but I had not carefully reviewed them before officiating at this particular wedding. I remember the first two points. I stumbled my way through the third and totally forgot the fourth. What was the problem? It wasn't that I didn't know what I wanted to say. It wasn't that I hadn't prepared. It was simply that I was over-confident. I wasn't nervous enough. I had never, even for a moment, thought that I couldn't handle that situation. I was simply over-confident.

A certain elderly pastor used to tell this story. A good many years ago an alcoholic in the town where he was pastor was converted and joined his church. In the old days before his conversion he used to ride into town almost every day and hitch his horse to a certain post in front of the corner saloon. After his conversion, in spite of repeated warnings from his faithful pastor, he still hitched up his horse to the same hitching post. At last he fell into his old drinking habit and, according to the customs of that day, was tried and expelled from the church. What was the secret of his downfall? It was over-confidence. He needed to pray, 'And lead me not into temptation but deliver me from the evil one.' He needed to personalize the Lord's Prayer and then prove his sincerity by getting a new hitching post as far away from the saloon as possible. Those of us who pray about temptation, pray realizing our own weakness. God's Word says:

> *If you think you are standing firm, be careful that you don't fall!*
>
> 1 Cor. 10:12

God will Make us Conquerors

We are privileged to have the conviction that the victory can be ours. Jesus knows all about us. He completely and perfectly understands us.

> *We have a great high priest who has gone through the heavens, Jesus the Son of God, let us hold firmly to the faith we profess. For we do not have a high priest who is unable to sympathize with our weaknesses, but we have one who has been tempted in every way, just as we are – yet without sin. Let us then approach the throne of grace with confidence, so that we may receive mercy and find grace to help us in our time of need.*
>
> Heb. 4:14-16

Jesus is victor. He has provided a way of escape. He has made it possible for us to endure our temptation. We can come through it victoriously. This can be our conviction, that

God will either give us the strength to face a test, or use that test to increase our strength.

When we look closely at the pattern of Jesus' life, we see His refusal to misuse His wonderful powers for selfish ends. That challenges me to a greater stewardship of my resources. Satan tried to get Him to look out for His own comfort - hungry as He was - by turning stones to bread. Religion to Jesus wasn't a way to simply feel good all the time. Satan tempted Him to make a great display of His divine powers by leaping from that pinnacle. Jesus models for us that religion is more than a stage for self-display. Satan offered Him all political power. Let's never forget that Satan has that right. Because He is the prince of this world, He can offer us a kingdom. Jesus refused it - for His kingdom was in eternity. And so are yours and mine.

So when we pray this prayer, as forgiven and forgiving persons, we pray it with the conviction that sin is deadly, that we are weak and vulnerable, but Jesus can turn our potential defeat into victory as we're empowered by His Holy Spirit.

This is a Prayer for Deliverance

Luke quotes Jesus as saying only, 'And lead us not into temptation' (Luke 11:4). Matthew remembers Jesus adding these additional words,

'… but deliver us from the evil one' (Matt. 6:13). This prayer calls for deliverance that only a leader can provide.

It implies a negative leadership as we are to pray that God will not lead us into that which will destroy us, whether it be by allowing a test that is too hard for us to endure or by allowing us to stumble unguided into an area of seduction that can destroy us. His leadership is not negative. 'Lead us not into temptation!' By no means do we want to get near that which will destroy us. And it's a prayer that cries out for positive leadership. 'Deliver us from the evil one!' That's what we want. That's what we need. We need a Deliverer. We need one who goes before us as a cloud by day and a pillar of fire by night. How amazing is God's deliverance. In what magnificent ways He answers these honest prayers.

God's desire is to release us from bondage. Some of us are locked into impossible situations. Our lives are being destroyed by sin in its blatant, fleshy form or its much more subtle, spiritual captivity. Sin is sin. Bondage is bondage. And bondage is so debilitating. Yet God has the capacity to deliver us from bondage. His deliverance may come in dramatic ways, or it may come much more quietly. The Lord uses a strange turn of events, a sudden insight, a book, sermon or conversation that suddenly cut us free from sin's ropes that hold us in bondage.

Deliverance comes not only by releasing us from bondage; it also comes by holding us faithful, which is something just as beautiful. If only we would allow Him, God would deliver us from sin by saving us from ever becoming debilitated by it. He has the capacity to take hold of people in the sweet innocence of their youth and hold them in His care until the end of their lives.

The evangelist Gypsy Smith used to tell of a testimony meeting he attended many years ago in his church in England. A drunkard told how God had saved him from the gutter. A man who had served time in prison told how he had been rescued from a life of crime. Another said that he had ridden about the city with the Lord Mayor but had also had to beg bread from door to door. One after another told such stories until Gypsy Smith could stand it no longer. He sprang to his feet, crying, 'The Lord has done great things for you, but he has done far greater for me. He saved me from going astray. He has kept me from my youth!'

God's amazing grace can deliver the prodigal out of sin's bondage back into the embrace of his loving Father. But isn't it even more wonderful when the potential prodigal is kept from ever going into the far country, than when God delivers us from sin's slavery? Better still, He delivers us from the tragedy of wasted lives. We should thank God that Jesus has taught us to pray, 'And lead us not into temptation, but deliver us from the evil one.' This is a prayer for deliverance.

Ascription of praise

And we should also thank God for the ascription of praise that some of the ancient manuscripts add:

> *For Yours is the kingdom and the power and the glory forever. Amen.*
>
> Matt. 6:13

In these words Jesus incorporated the affirmation given by David:

> *Yours, O Lord, is the greatness and the power and the glory and the majesty and the splendor, for everything in heaven and earth is Yours. Yours, O Lord, is the kingdom; You are exalted as head over all.*
>
> 1 Chron. 29:11

It is restated by Paul:

The Lord will rescue me from every evil attack and will bring me safely to His heavenly kingdom. To Him be glory for ever and ever, Amen.

2 Tim. 4:18

We are empowered in the face of temptation by the very God who is King of Kings, who is all-powerful, and who deserves all the glory for ever and ever.

To Know or to Do

How serious are we about prayer? It's one thing to have mastered the teaching about the Lord's Prayer, but it's another thing to pray. It's one thing to be able to quote all the Bible references and the importance of prayer and the promises God has given to answer our prayers, it's still another thing to pray.

Calvin Miller, in his book titled *Tables of Inwardness*, writes these words:

Once we become masters of our schedules, we will be able to approach God in peace. Those who have not learned this come to God as they do everything else… late! They rush into His presence a tornado of hurriedness. They blurt out their confessions and whisk off to the next appointment, glad that they have managed to work God into their blustery schedules.

141

It is easier to talk about prayer than to pray. It is easier to master the teachings of the Scriptures about prayer than to actually take the time to pray. Those men and women who not only know about prayer but take the time to pray are privileged indeed.

The Family you Want

How to Establish an Authentic, Loving home

John A. Huffman Jr.

Whilst we all have a deep longing to be part of an ideal family, imperfect people make imperfect ones – it's a simple fact of life. Should we, as some in our post-modern society suggest, just give up?

If that thought depresses you then take heart and let John Huffman help you to achieve the best family you can. It won't be perfect but it will be better.

'With wisdom and winsomeness John has give us a book that can strengthen families and grow trust and love. I heartily recommend this book.'

Jill Briscoe

'His approach is thoughtful, his style clear... this book is authentic.'

Leighton Ford

'An excellent reference book for young people setting out on the adventure of life, for married couples seeking help in dealing with problems or for Ministers involved in counselling in extended family situations.'

The Monthly Record

'here is healing medicine for all who care about the family'
Harold Myra

ISBN 1-85792-933-0

Christian Focus Publications

publishes books for all ages

Our mission statement –

STAYING FAITHFUL

In dependence upon God we seek to help make His infallible Word, the Bible, relevant. Our aim is to ensure that the Lord Jesus Christ is presented as the only hope to obtain forgiveness of sin, live a useful life and look forward to heaven with Him.

REACHING OUT

Christ's last command requires us to reach out to our world with His gospel. We seek to help fulfill that by publishing books that point people towards Jesus and help them develop a Christ-like maturity. We aim to equip all levels of readers for life, work, ministry and mission.

Books in our adult range are published in three imprints.

Christian Focus contains popular works including biographies, commentaries, basic doctrine and Christian living. Our children's books are also published in this imprint.

Mentor focuses on books written at a level suitable for Bible College and seminary students, pastors, and other serious readers. The imprint includes commentaries, doctrinal studies, examination of current issues and church history.

Christian Heritage contains classic writings from the past.

Christian Focus Publications, Ltd
Geanies House, Fearn, Ross-shire,
IV20 1TW, Scotland, United Kingdom
info@christianfocus.com
www.christianfocus.com